Who Am I, Really?

How Our Wounds Can Lead to Healing

Who Am I, Really?

How Our Wounds Can Lead to Healing

by Joseph Cavanaugh

Foreword by Brother David Steindl-Rast

Underwood Books
Nevada City, California
2004

Who Am I, Really?
How Our Wounds Can Lead to Healing
ISBN 1-887424-89-X

"A Network for Grateful Living (ANGeL) is a global network of individuals, organizations, and communities exploring the transformative power of gratefulness in personal lives and as the core inspiration for sustainable activism in areas of universal concern, including interfaith work, social justice, economics, politics, and ecology. ANGeL's interactive website— **www.gratefulness.org**—a free public resource, connects people around the world whose spiritual practice is grateful living. Books can be ordered on the site through Amazon.com, which helps support ANGeL." —*Brother David Steindl-Rast*

Distributed to the trade by Publisher Group West
800-788-3123

10 9 8 7 6 5 4 2 1
First Edition

This book is dedicated to my mentor, teacher,
and most of all my friend,
Brother David Steindl-Rast,
a true exemplar of gratefulness and great-*full*-ness.

Acknowledgments

I would like to express my gratitude to all of the staff at Esalen Institute for their support in providing space for my workshops, without which this book may never have been conceived.

I am grateful to my wife Carol, whose feedback and suggestions were essential in formulating the ideas presented in this book; my daughter Shanti, for her editing expertise; my daughter Jackie, for her patience with my short attention span while teaching me how to use the computer; and to my son Joey, whose natural gift for cartooning has always been an inspiration to me. If I were able to even come close to his expertise and talent, I might someday feel comfortable calling myself a cartoonist.

My warmest regards go to the following who took the time to review and critique my manuscript before it went to print: Brother David Steindl-Rast, PhD, OSB; Jeff Kane, MD; Helen Crawford, MD; Charles Sternberg, MD; Rich McCutchan, PhD; Hank Snavely, PhD; Steve Sheridan, MFT; William Larsen, MFT.

I would also like to thank the staff at Flour Garden Bakery in Grass Valley, most of whom know my "non-fat, hot chocolate, super-hot, no-foam, no-whip" drink by heart. While typing my manuscript, their warm-hearted generosity kindled my spirits and kept me motivated when I felt stuck on a sentence or paragraph.

I am indebted to my editor, Kyle Roderick, who went out of her way to offer feedback, provide resources, and suggest critical changes that would enhance the quality of the material presented in this book.

Finally, I want to express my deepest appreciation for my publisher, Tim Underwood, who had enough confidence and faith in my work to offer it for publication. Without his on-going encouragement, support, and optimistic attitude, this project would never have come to fruition.

Table of Contents

Part Three: Self-Acceptance—The Heart of Healing

Foreword

by Brother David Steindl-Rast

What do you admire more, astute insight or the ability to teach? You do not have to choose. Joe Cavanaugh is blessed with both these gifts, and he blesses you in turn with this book. He puts a key to self-understanding in your hand.

How does he teach? Effortlessly: by making us laugh; by distilling his lessons into cartoons. It all seems so simple. Yet it goes deep. There is layer upon layer of insight underneath that simplicity.

By typing "power of ten" into the browser window of your computer, you can link to one of the most intriguing features on the Internet. Starting with a view of deep space, each successive frame is reduced by the power of ten to show our galaxy, our solar system, our earth, a section of its surface, and so on, until a leaf is reduced to cells, to their molecular structure, atoms, and finally to subatomic particles and their mysterious dance which resembles the dance of galaxies in the universe and so brings us full circle. Joe Cavanaugh's *Who Am I, Really?* also leads us on a thrilling exploration that ends where it began: He starts with the widest vision of consciousness, explains how we get entangled in the human drama, and shows us the way back to the source from which we came—a consciousness that is our true identity, a consciousness synonymous with love.

On the way we gain insights into topics that vitally concern each of us in our search for true identity: fear, and how it comes about; self-esteem and its foundations; alienation; helplessness and depression; as well as the healing power of self-awareness, self-acceptance, and forgiveness.

9

Here is an author who speaks the language of common sense, and so he touches a common chord in his readers' hearts. His touch is a healing touch. The gift I admire most in Joe Cavanaugh is the passion and compassion of a healer. May this book make his healing touch reach a world in need of healing.

Living on a Wounded Planet . . .
An Introduction

"Life is suffering."
—Buddha

This book was inspired by people like you; people who feel deeply and who are discovering that life's journey can paradoxically wound us and heal us. If you are committed to your own growth and willing to embrace the dragons of personal wounds and trauma, you can heal your past, transform your present and ensure yourself a more peaceful future. You will experience greater vitality, creativity and passion in your life and your relationships. You will discover the transfomative power of love.

Working with thousands of people over the years through teaching, facilitating workshops and as a therapist, I noticed that a common wound is the source of most human suffering. This is the simplest and most fundamental wound we human beings can experience—the betrayal of love, the wounding of our heart.

I am not referring exclusively to the pain and loss that naturally accompanies a failed romance or friendship. I am speaking instead of betrayal in the largest sense of the word, the pervasive losses associated with being a human on planet earth. This betrayal of love manifests in myriad forms. As children or adults, we may have experienced abuse, abandonment or deception at the hands of others. Or we may wound ourselves through excessive self-criticism and self-disapproval. We might have become self-abusive through the use of alcohol, drugs, or engaging in other addictive behaviors. These are all forms of self-abandonment.

TRANSCENDENTAL BABY

Another form of betrayal, even more fundamental to our human existence, stems from the sorrow that accompanies the inevitable loss, separation and death of those people and things we care about most. And, of course, we must all come to grips with the *ultimate* loss—our own mortality. All of these represent forms of loss that are fundamental to our existence. They come with living on an exquisitely precious yet wounded planet, a world of light and dark, life, death and rebirth.

Paradoxically, if you are incapable of acknowledging and grieving your losses, you will never experience the *joy* that comes with embracing to the fullest life's agonies and ecstasies. Joy and sorrow are not mutually exclusive. Rather, they are intricately linked together in a bond of reciprocity, just as are the cycles of day and night, and the seasons of the year. Joy and sorrow harmoniously coexist just as daylight shares the earth with nightfall, and summer with winter. If you deny one, you automatically deny yourself the other. This cosmic paradox is forever casting its shadow upon the journey of awakening.

While in the midst of pain and suffering, it is all too easy to become cynical and lose faith in the *spiritual* dimensions of Consciousness, dimensions that lie just beyond the reach of our immediate perception. Because life may fall short of our demands and expectations doesn't mean these other realities don't exist, anymore than not seeing ultra-violet or infrared with our naked eye precludes their existence. These realities simply *transcend* our personal struggles altogether. As Confucius wrote, "The greatest obstacle to seeing is the eye, the greatest obstacle to hearing, the ear."

Therefore, we must be careful never to throw out the transcendental baby with the waters of loss, sorrow and suffering that flow through our lives on a wounded planet.

Beneath the polarities of joy and sorrow resides the eternal, unchanging stillness of the Loving Heart. It is my strongest conviction that love is the fountainhead from which all of our joy springs forth, the fundamental principle underlying the entire universe. Love is the true *Essence* of *all* of us, from the most corrupt and sinister to the most benevolent and kind-hearted.

Reflect for a moment on the possibility that *all* of life's experiences play pivotal roles in the cosmic drama that unfolds before our eyes and in our hearts daily. Think of how Judas's betrayal of Jesus fulfilled the prophecy of a drama unfolding during that epic time in history. That prophecy *was* a betrayal of love.

I am not suggesting that we are all equally in touch with this deeper essence. That would mean that Jesus and Judas, or Gandhi and Hitler for that matter, were functioning at the same level of awareness. That was obviously not the case. Accessing this love is what the journey of awakening is all about— expanding our awareness, opening our hearts and developing the capacity to fully embrace the consciousness of love.

Today, on our besieged planet, we are each faced with the challenge of resurrecting our *own* Loving Heart, a flame that powers the core of our being. Yet, even if we know this, we may still feel a full range of emotions—anger, fear, hurt, and sadness—when we experience a loss. It is natural to feel pain if we lose someone—or something—dear to us. It is *still* necessary to grieve and integrate these losses, regardless of our level of awakening and spiritual maturity. We are still *human.*

This reminds me of a story about a respected monk and spiritual teacher who one afternoon was strolling through the garden of the ashram where he taught. He saw one of his students sitting on a rock in obvious pain, sobbing profusely. The monk approached him and asked, "What is wrong, my son, how can I help you?" The student looked sadly at his teacher and said, "My mother just died!" Consoling the student, the monk reminded him of the transcendental nature of reality; how death is simply a transition from the body into higher realms of spirit where all is eternally well and perfect. Reassured, the student felt much better as he bowed, thanked his teacher, and went upon his way.

A few days later, the student entered the garden and saw his teacher sitting upon the same rock crying inconsolably. The student asked, "Oh great teacher, you look so distraught, why are you crying?" "My mother just died," cried the monk. "But sir," exclaimed the student, "what about your words of wisdom, how you reassured me that all is perfect in the higher realms of spirit?" The monk looked sheepishly at his student and replied, "Yes, but this was MY mother!"

Some people get lost in the drama of life, while others deny it altogether. The monk had not abandoned his commitment and devotion to a higher, transcendental reality. Yet being human, when he lost his mother, he felt compelled to shed tears. His actions modeled a profound truth to his student: Although there is *much* more to us than meets the eye, we are *still* human at the same time. This requires stepping back from our usual myopic perspective to grasp the bigger picture—a picture that is both *transcendent* and *immanent* simultaneously—a picture that both transcends and embraces our human struggle for awakening.

I wrote this book as an exploration of the human drama and dilemma we face when we lose touch with that larger perspective. This book is intended to cultivate insight into the nature of our true identity and our search for meaning and purpose. It is intended to assist in exploring some of the ways we hope to heal our wounds with wisdom and compassion. Although each chapter could have become a book in its own right, my intention was to write with simplicity. Oftentimes, less is more.

If a picture is worth a thousand words, a cartoon is worth a thousand pictures. The language of myth, metaphor, and storytelling has a way of penetrating the heart in a manner beyond words. Metaphor evokes the higher realms of imagination and bridges what is immanent and what is transcendent. The same can be true of images evoked through cartoons. Cartoons can provide comic relief while giving us permission to laugh at ourselves. Cartoons lighten the burden of attachment that goes with taking life too seriously and allow us to glimpse the light that resides just beneath the veil of our personal drama.

The words and images in this book are meant to illuminate what happens when we lose touch with the deeper Essence of who we are, and the ensuing drama we create in our desperate search to reconnect with that Essence. Obviously the transcendent cannot be pointed at directly. Neither can the eye see itself. It is sometimes necessary to look with our *peripheral* vision to see the faint reflections of truth lying just beyond the threshold of our linear mind.

In Part One I invite you to set aside your beliefs and assumptions about reality, keeping your mind fresh with curiosity and wonder. As the Roman philosopher Epictetus once said, "It is impossible for a man to learn what he thinks he already knows." In our birth descent into matter, we forget who we are and lose touch with our true identity. This leads to fear and subsequent pursuit of a false identity as a means of creating value and purpose in our lives.

Through metaphors and images, we will briefly explore the origin of the universe from the perspective of various philosophers and mystics. The cartoons are meant to illustrate the journey that unfolds within each one of us as we walk our own personal path of awakening.

Part Two explores the influence our early childhood has on our search for identity. Love is important in developing a positive self-image and a cohesive sense of self. Without a solid foundation of support and nurturing from our primary caregivers, our self-esteem and confidence is impaired. If we are fortunate enough to have reasonable support from "good enough" parents, our burden may be lightened. We may not have experienced the same degree of hardship as those that were abused or neglected. However, none of us get through life unscathed. We have all experienced some degree of emotional pain from loss, separation or betrayal in our lifetime.

We can easily become attached to things and situations in an attempt to lessen our pain. They provide temporary relief and comfort by distracting us from the issues we don't want to face. But attachments often produce the opposite of what we intend. They can become a burden, demanding our undivided attention and maintenance. This can leave us feeling helpless and out of control, creating a *self-perpetuating* cycle of depression and self-defeating behavior. At that point, we may be forced to seek ways to break the cycle of despair. We either continue suffering or find ways to heal our wounds and discover who we really are.

Part Three addresses the tools and dynamics necessary to facilitate healing: self-awareness, self-acceptance, and the ability to take positive action—to fully *live* and *feel* our vision each moment. Self-acceptance is critical to the healing process and functions as the heart of healing. It modulates the degree to which self-awareness and action operate in a positive manner in our lives. Grieving our past losses nurtures hope for the future and breaks the cycle of depression. Forgiveness plays a crucial role in letting go of our past as we develop empathy and compassion for ourselves and others.

The path of compassion will lead us back to the *source* from which we came; our True Identity as *Psyche*, or Soul. The essence of the soul is *loving*. Our path to healing will lead us back to simply becoming *what we already are*: love.

We shall not cease from exploration and the end of
all our exploration will be to arrive where we first
started and know that place for the first time.
        — T.S. Eliot

To set the stage for our human drama to unfold, we need to start *prior* to the beginning:

Prior to the beginning...Imagine a state of absolute still-ness. In this state, nothing (no-"*thing*") is present, just pure, formless, emptiness. Imagine this undifferentiated state as existing prior to time, space, matter and form—a still-point from which all else will eventually emerge. Like a calm motionless pond on a moonlit night, this undisturbed stillness is in a state of perfect harmony and balance. Imagine and feel this moonlit pond as the still waters of *love*, the essence of all Creation, in a Non-dual state of infinite potential.

Essence is emptiness...everything else accidental.
Emptiness brings peace to loving...everything else, disease.
In this world of trickery, emptiness is what your soul wants.
          —Rumi

Imagine this stillness as the essence of your soul, the sanctity of soul where your heart longs to return. While embarking upon the journey of Consciousness from wound-ing to healing, trust your feelings, allow your heart to be your guide. The path of the heart takes great courage, and the word courage is derived from the Latin root *cor*, mean-ing heart. This book can provide a road map into the heart, leading you back to the embrace of your True Self, which is simply *love*.

IN THE BEGINNING...

PART ONE
The Beginning...

In that deep force, the last fact behind which analysis cannot go, all things find their common origin. It is one light which beams out of a thousand stars. It is one soul which animates all.

—Ralph Waldo Emerson

1

One Consciousness

There is, at the surface, infinite variety of things;
at the center there is simplicity and unity of cause.
—Ralph Waldo Emerson

In the beginning…The primordial stillness began to stir, generating a powerful and magnificent force. This mysterious pulse created a gentle ripple upon the surface. The ripple multiplied, generating more energy, motion, and eventually matter. These ripples increased exponentially, creating the image of time and space; the solar system; our planets and all that we have come to know as "reality."

The late quantum physicist and cosmologist, David Bohm, described the immensity of this primal force as a pulse of cosmic energy rising and falling like the waves of the ocean. The low point of each wave he referred to as the "zero point," a point where the energy is so minimal it appears as nothing but still, empty space. Paradoxically, according to Bohm, the sum of this "emptiness" is so enormous it approaches absolute *fullness*. It is comprised of such immense and powerful energy that one gentle ripple from this macroscopic force appears as a "big bang" from our microscopic vantage point—a "bang" that continues reverberating fifteen billion years later!

Bohm's description of the universe is amazingly similar to the Taoist principle of "emptiness," the "still-point" from which the universe emerged. The great mystery of creation still fascinates mystics, philosophers, and scientists today. Albert Einstein, a philosopher and humanitarian as well as a physicist, reminded us that "The greatest thing we can experience is the mysterious." Each moment represents a new mystery unfolding before our eyes. Eleanor Roosevelt summarized it well: "Yesterday is history, tomorrow is a mystery, today is a gift." If you are present to receive the gift of the moment, you can actively participate in unraveling the mystery of your own soul. Dancing on the edge of the mysterious will open you to an exciting world of wonder and awe.

"Reality" is merely the world of forms, accessible to us through our five senses. Underlying these forms lies the Eternal Formless Reality of Love, which remains the source of all creation. Love is the primal force from which all else came into being. It is the original pulse of which all else in the known universe is merely a *reflection*.

Author, international lecturer and teacher of *A Course in Miracles*, Marianne Williamson tells us "love isn't material, it is energy…it isn't seen with the physical eyes or heard with the physical ears…" We also know from quantum physics that the fundamental property of all matter is energy. So let's take a "quantum leap" and suggest that energy itself is synonymous with love, and that both energy and love are reflected through the evolution of Consciousness. Imagine, then, that Consciousness is the vehicle through which love is made manifest in the physical world, expressed through such qualities as acceptance, kindness, empathy and compassion.

Love is the cohesive force through which everything else came into being, as well as the organizing principle seeking to unify what was torn asunder by its own original creative pulse. As Pierre Teilhard De Chardin wrote, "Driven by the forces of love, the fragments of the world seek each other so that the world may come into being."

Mystics often refer to this "coming into being" as "involution," the descent of spirit into matter. "Evolution," on the other hand, refers to the "return" to our original state prior to the original pulse. Consciousness is the means through which evolution occurs. This One Consciousness descends into the world of form as the vehicle of evolution, the vehicle through which love manifests in the world.

Consciousness, referred to in this manner, will be illustrated with a capital "C," as opposed to the state of simply being "conscious" or "unconscious" per se, which will be indicated with a small "c."

Why would this "Creative Pulse" occur, and then seek to reunite what it had itself separated? There is no easy answer. Philosophers, mystics and scientists have been contemplating this "koan" for centuries. This "Primal Paradox," the "Original Sin" of Creation, may be beyond the comprehension of the linear mind. We often gain insight into these questions through metaphor, parable and imagery, and hopefully, through cartoons as well.

Ask yourself what would happen if you lived as though there is only One Consciousness, and that is Love. Imagine that the micro-world of subatomic particles and the macro-world of interstellar space; that single-celled protozoan and multicellular organisms—from the cell to the Soul—are all manifestations of this One Consciousness evolving through the world of form. Imagine living your life as though love is the organizing Principle, the thread that weaves its way through the fabric of our entire universe.

2

Veil of Forgetfulness

One dog barks at a shadow, a thousand dogs take it for reality.
—Chinese Proverb

As this Consciousness of Love, or Soul, descends into the physical plane, matter is created and the physical world of form becomes what we call reality.

When matter comes into being, light is reflected *from* matter, creating a world of shadows. The *veil of forgetfulness* descends upon Consciousness, and the world of duality—the world of reflected light and darkness—prevails. Consciousness becomes *unconscious* of itself, residing in the world of shadows. Evolution has begun. Living creatures slowly begin to emerge from these shadows, leading eventually to human beings.

But how can "something" come from "nothing"? Let's take a look. The word "reality" is from the Latin word *res*, meaning "*matter*" or "*thing.*" If the fundamental property of all matter is energy, then reality ("*matter*" or "*thing*") comes from no-matter (no-"*thing*")! Looking out into the world of things (reality), we identify with them, taking these things as the substance of our own existence—a simple case of mistaken identity. We now see the world of *reflected images* as the measure of all things.

As you may know, the Hindu word *Maya* is commonly interpreted as "illusion," "magic," or "appearance." The literal translation, however, is related to the Sanskrit root *ma*, used in everyday words such as "matter," "mother," and "measure." Referring to Maya as an "illusion" is only partially truthful. It would be more accurate to say Maya is the "measure of all things," the reference point from which we look out into our universe, the world of matter, which we take for reality. And *that* in turn is an illusion, or possibly even a collective hallucination! At best, it represents the collective *identity crisis* at the root of human suffering.

The "world of appearances" is eloquently portrayed in Plato's Allegory of the Cave. Born in the 5th century before Christ, Plato was the famous Greek philosopher who founded *The Academy* outside of Athens, Greece. He played a pivotal role in establishing the philosophical roots of western thinking and the study of human consciousness.

Plato portrayed human beings as being shackled inside a cave, facing towards the back wall, away from the light shining in from the opening of the cave. Upon that wall, humans see reflected images, the shadows of the people walking past them from behind, and they mistake these shadows for the people themselves. When one person finally breaks free of the shackles and finds his way out of the cave into the light, he is at first stunned, blinded and disoriented. However, he gradually adjusts and is filled with rapture and awe from his clear vision of the light. Rushing back down into the cave to awaken others to the truth, he is again confused by the darkness; he stumbles and becomes disoriented. His peers scoff at him and distrust his sanity, eventually killing him for disturbing their version of reality.

Our collective identity crisis is described by many mystical traditions as the "illusion of separation," a deep spiritual wound. Our personality (persona) reflects the masks we wear and the roles we play as we carry out our own personal drama within this great illusion of separation. And *play* it is...the word "illusion" itself is Latin, meaning, "to play."

So, the veil of forgetfulness, the illusion of separation, sets the stage for the human drama. Like participants in a cosmic game of charades, we assume roles in the theater of life—a land of fantasy. We get caught up in this drama and confuse it with reality. The stage upon which we play out these archetypal dramas is Planet Earth. The depth psychologist and poet of the human soul, Carl Jung befittingly proclaimed, "We meet ourselves time and time again in a thousand disguises on the path of life."

Imagine that if the world is always a *reflection* of One Consciousness, and Plato's shadows are really *images* from the light of this Consciousness, then we are not *really* separated, except in the fantasy of our own minds. Clinging to these fantasies keeps us wrapped in a veil of fear that perpetuates our suffering indefinitely. Our challenge is to free ourselves from the shackles of illusion by opening our hearts to the truth and experiencing the depth of our soul.

3

The World of Duality

*Out beyond ideas of rightdoing and wrongdoing, is a field.
I'll meet you there.*
            —Rumi

As you can see, we live in a world where we only glimpse the *reflected images* of a Greater Reality, and mistake the one for the other. In order to *see* these images, there must be a separation of the *seer* from *that which is seen*, a separation of the *subject* from the *object seen*. This primary dualism characterizes a world now polarized into "day and night," "wrong and right," "black and white," and so on.

Philosophers and religious scholars worldwide have addressed the dualistic nature of physical reality. Dualism has been alluded to in myth and fairy tales around the world from antiquity. The depth psychologist, Carl Jung, used the terms Animus and Anima for the masculine and feminine principles contained within the human psyche. Taoists called them Yang and Yin; Hindus called them Shiva and Shakti, while Christians refer to them as Adam and Eve. This underlying principle of duality reflects the "splitting" of Consciousness into *Subject* and *Object*.

29

Plato refers to dualism in his story of the powerful mythic god, Zeus, who, in a fit of rage, split human beings in half. We have since run around, Plato says, seeking union with our "split-apart," our other half, in order to become whole once again. Jung taught that we each seek to unify the unconscious polarity of masculine and feminine within ourselves through relationships. Your relationships, then, become a common ground through which you seek balance and harmony and wholeness.

When we come into this world, we are already pre-wired to some degree—we are not just "blank slates." As you may already know, to a certain extent, biological laws dictate the story of your life. Evolutionary biologists refer to these laws as *genetics*. Neuropsychologists describe *neuropathways*, *neurotransmitters* and *synapses* in the brain; mystics may refer to these influences as being *multidimensional* (from past lives). Jung spoke of the *collective unconscious*, a repository of the collective experiences of humanity, which is accessed by or carried within our psyche (soul). It doesn't matter which reference point you adopt. What matters most is recognizing how these influences might unconsciously impact your choices and behavior.

Additionally, our lives are shaped by our current life experiences. An acorn becomes an oak tree through genetic necessity, but its health depends on how well it is situated; on the degree of shade and sunlight it is exposed to, and the nourishment it receives from its environment. Like the acorn, we come in to this world with a specific genetic pre-disposition. We are then shaped, molded and conditioned by the beliefs, morals and values of the society—and family—to which we are exposed. Our attitudes, beliefs and perceptions about "reality" are solidly anchored in place at about the age of five. As we develop into adulthood, these attitudes and beliefs are relegated to the unconscious. They have a powerful influence over how we think, feel and act, as well as the choices we make in life.

As a therapist, I worked with a client who grew up in a family of chaos and was exposed to drinking, fighting and general upheaval throughout her entire childhood. She simply assumed her life was "normal," and "that's just the way things were." She had an abusive father who continually belittled her, telling her how worthless she was and that she would never amount to anything. Her self-esteem had been shattered, leaving her feeling inadequate and worthless. As an adult, she found herself attracted to men who treated her with the same disrespect as had her father. She confessed to feeling "uncomfortable" and "undeserving" if a man treated her kindly; she was never attracted to those men. She wasn't interested in them because they fell outside of her comfort zone, her template of love. She had no reference point for healthy love. Consequently, she settled for what was safe and familiar even though it perpetuated her pain and suffering.

Our early immediate environment is our reference point for reality. If we grew up under a rain cloud, we may never know that just behind the veil of the cloud the sun is brightly shining. In other words, *our perception of reality is limited to, and defined by, the context in which we experience this reality*—"we don't know what we don't know!"

Our job is to find balance in the midst of polarity. Not only do we struggle with, we often seem forced to choose between "right versus wrong," "good versus bad," or even "God versus the Devil!" If our morals are conflicted over these polarities, the gap is widened between who we really are and who we think we "ought" to be. The result is shame, guilt, fear and self-doubt. These feelings cause frustration, stifle our creativity and deaden our spirit.

The influences of our distant and immediate past are powerful forces. We must acknowledge, accept and integrate these experiences. One sign of emotional maturity is the *ability to live with uncertainty and ambiguity*. If you are *conscious* of how your past influences your present life, you are in a better position to deal with the uncertainty that goes with living in a world of constant change. You are more likely to make choices that positively impact the direction of your present and future.

I worked with a young man who grew up in an alcoholic family. He himself started drinking at an early age as a way of coping with life's uncertainties. When he realized he was following in his dad's footsteps, he sought therapy. By recognizing and working with his limitations, his fears and insecurities, he was able to establish clear boundaries around his use of alcohol, and learned to cope with stress and anxiety in a healthy manner. His past no longer controlled his future.

We are not simply victims of our genetic coding and childhood conditioning. If we were, we might as well throw in the towel—or dump Prozac into our drinking water to numb our collective pain.

If we were merely casualties of our past, there would be no reason to seek help or challenge our boundaries. We would lose all hope for the future and remain confined by our assumed limitations. Darkness breeds fear, and our fear is rooted in ignorance—we can't see clearly in the dark.

4

Fear—The Biggest Fantasy of All

A person cannot depend on his eyes when his Imagination is out of focus.
         —Mark Twain

We live in the world of reflection—*images*—of that which is transcendent. We don't know *what* we don't know, and we don't know *that* we don't know. Ignorance breeds fear. Our fears are then magnified by our *imagination*, stranding us in a house of crooked mirrors and distorted images. Fear increases the level of the stress hormone cortisol in our body, causing chronic tension and anxiety. This tension impairs our ability to think clearly and perform at an optimal level of creativity.

As children, where I grew up in San Francisco, we used to tell "spooky" nighttime stories to one another for fun. As the evening progressed, our imaginations took over and tension would build inside us. Before long we started hearing noises, we even saw things moving in the dark. Soon we were running through the house, slamming closet doors to fend off attacks by ghostly creatures. This game went on for what seemed like hours—we were fully absorbed in our imaginary world and actually began to believe it was true. Basically, we were hallucinating.

Psychologists and human performance experts tell us that the unconscious cannot discern between real or imagined input. We "think" in pictures, an evolutionary tool anchored in place long before we developed the skill of a symbolic language. In a sense, we live in our own imaginary world and are directing and starring in our own personal movie, which no one else ever sees!

Our behavior will be consistent with what we imagine to be true about ourselves, and the world around us. "Where your mind goes, your body is soon to follow." I have worked with many clients whose nervous systems have gone awry simply by *talking* about past experiences of abuse or trauma. They start to sweat, their heart races, their palms sweat, they may even begin to cry. Their unconscious is not differentiating between past, present or future. They experience the past in the present, while simultaneously rehearsing the future. They reinforce fear in their imagination as they talk, putting their body in a state of "alert" to protect themselves from "danger" looming ahead."

Living in the world of duality, we forget who we are and the love that resides at our core. We develop survival strategies, elaborate defenses to protect ourselves from danger and from our own personal ghosts in the closet. These defenses foster further separation, loneliness and despair.

The more elaborate our defenses become, the more we focus on *differences* rather than *similarities*. We begin seeing "ghosts in the closet" and mistake them for reality. These ghosts breed hostility, rooted in fear, rooted in ignorance. We start fighting over differences. We go to war to prove "we" are right and "they" are wrong. The earthly battle of duality, in the name of "Good versus Evil" becomes magnified beyond proportion. We are left more alone, desperate, and afraid. It is as though one of the "l's" in "all-one" fell

into this crack of despair, leaving us "a-lone," trying to figure out where in the "I" we are!

Living in this world of reflected images distorts our vision and alters our perception of reality. It impacts our *self*-image, self-esteem and personal identity. In a vain attempt to find an acceptable identity, we distort our self-image even further. We try to live up to the values and expectations of our culture and we measure our self-worth by how well we fit in—how we should act; how we should feel; how we should look; how we should dress—and it is *never* good enough.

We lose when we compromise our own truth to meet the demands of others, when we compare ourselves to others to determine our value and worth. We can only be who we *are*, no matter how hard we try to resist our true nature.

Or, if we are deeply entrenched in our defenses, we may deny there is a problem, disconnect from our inner self, and remain comforted by the bliss of ignorance. Or, as James Joyce wrote, "Mr. Duffy lives just a short distance from his body." We look the other way

and cry out, "Problem? What problem?" We ask this not because we have *overcome* our struggles, but instead, we simply pretend they don't exist. We alter our perception to avoid dealing with the pain of separation, and our images of the world and ourselves become distorted. Desperately attempting to make things appear better than they really are, we rationalize our pain away and live in a "happy" state of denial.

In order to deal with a problem, we first need to acknowledge that there *is* a problem. Ignorance may be "bliss," but *awareness* is freedom. At some point, we may feel overwhelmed by our pain and loneliness. In order to grow and find peace of mind, we are compelled to ponder the vexing question, "Who am I, *really*? And the quest begins.

As your quest unfolds, you may find yourself looking squarely into the eyes of the dragon, and behind its gaze you will see a reflection of the challenges that lay before you. This may seem unsettling and even frightening to you at times, which is a good thing. This unsettledness will arouse your emotions and stir your spirit, goading you along your path of awakening. By simply trusting the wisdom of your heart, your fears will be transformed into an adventure in experiencing the mystery of your own soul.

PART TWO
The Human Drama

Dreams are real while they last. Can we say more of life?
—Havelock Ellis

5

The Quest for Knowledge—
A Search for Identity

All men by nature desire to know.
　　　—Aristotle

Only human beings can contemplate the nature of reality and ponder such abstract questions as Shakespeare's "To be or not to be?" The instinct to know, to reflect on the meaning of life or where we came from, is as fundamental to human consciousness as all other instincts. An "instinct to know?" Exactly what does this mean? Contemporary scholars don't commonly refer to the quest for knowledge as an "instinct." Instincts are generally relegated to survival motives, such as the acquisition of food, water and shelter. Biologists humorously refer to these instincts as the "famous four F's of survival"—fight, flight, food, and sex!"

The founder of Psychoanalysis, Sigmund Freud, elaborated on *two* of these instincts in detail: our "sexual and aggressive" instincts. These instincts are important. They are essential for survival, and are related to the primitive, "reptilian" part of your brain located in the brain stem. But you are not a lizard. If you were, you might eat your offspring for breakfast and that would be the end of it. "To be *eaten* or not to be *eaten*" is as profound as things get for a lizard—to live or to die.

As Consciousness evolved, so did our brains. Contemporary research in human development provides indisputable evidence that mammals, especially humans, have an instinct for emotional and social bonding. I admit it seems there are a lot of lizards running around in drag as human beings. But for the most part, rather than eat our offspring for breakfast, our instinct is to nurture them and protect them from harm. In the narrow sense of the word, we feel *love* for them.

Contact, touch and close connection with others is known to enhance the functioning of the immune system in human beings. In their book, *A General Theory of Love*, Thomas Lewis, M.D., Fari Amini, M.D. and Richard Lannon, M.D. state that some mammals, when isolated for as little as thirty minutes, show up to a six-fold increase in the amount of cortisol, a primary stress hormone, in their bloodstream. They also emphasize the powerful influence that contact, nurturing and bonding has in the healthy development of infants and young children. The bonding instinct is a byproduct of the development of the second part of the brain, the *limbic*, or *mammalian* brain. The mammalian brain is the seat of your emotions. It has a powerful influence over how you feel about yourself and others, as well as your capacity to form lasting relationships. The issue here is, "to be *nurtured* or not to be *nurtured!*"

Evolution, like Consciousness, is in perpetual motion. Most animals, once their basic instincts are met (food and safety), sink into quiet repose, like a cat curled up on the warm hood of a car. Human beings, on the other hand, would more likely be found looking *under* the hood of that car, seeing how it is built and what makes it run. We seem to have an inborn intellectual curiosity, a creative urge, to explore the environment for reasons other than hunting down a rodent for our next meal.

Human beings, it seems, are blessed with the instinctive urge to *know*—to explore, to learn, to create and to *understand*—the world around them. We do, as Aristotle pointed out, "desire to know," to discover who we are and where we came from. This desire is critical to the further evolution of Consciousness. If we did not satisfy it, we

would deprive ourselves of the essential ingredients for healthy growth and development.

You love your offspring. Rather than eat them, most likely you want to help them acquire the *best* education they can. Curiosity and intellectual hunger come primarily with the development of the newest part of the brain, your *neo-cortex*, which is most sophisticated in human beings. It is via the cortex that you have the potential to compose music, design houses, and solve complex mathematical problems. And when you do fall in love, it is your cortex that will wax poetically to touch the heart of your newly found beloved.

The instinctive quest for knowledge has manifested in many forms throughout history. Above the entrance to the Greek Temple of Delphi are inscribed the words, "Know Thyself." The word "Veda," from the ancient Hindu scriptures, is from the word, "*Vid*," meaning, "to know." In mythology, the ancient "Goddess of wisdom," *Sophia*, gave rise to the word *philosophy*: *philo (loving) Sophia (wisdom)*—hence, philosophy is "the love of wisdom or knowledge." In the Garden of Eden we find the *Tree of Knowledge of Good and Evil* (duality!). The name of an old sect of Christian mystics, the *Gnostics*, literally means "personal knowledge." The Buddha, when asked who he was, proclaimed, "I am awake!" "Buddha" is from the Sanskrit word *Bodhi*, meaning "awakened," "knowledge," or "enlightenment."

This fundamental instinct, the *desire to know*, is what drives you forward toward "wholeness." With the veil of forgetfulness securely in place, the fundamental question, "Who am I?" lingers on. Ironically, the wound of separation into the world of duality is the very wound that goads you along a path of awakening—desire becomes the agent of the soul. Intuitively, you know something has gone awry, something is missing, but you can't quite put your finger on what it is. This missing link goads your curiosity, and prompts your instinctive search for truth. If this urge toward fulfillment is thwarted, there are notable consequences. Intellectual starvation leads to a slow psychological death. The important question is, how was your search thwarted in the first place?

6

Guilt and Shame—
The Seeds of Despair

Most of us manage to survive childhood, but not all of us outgrow it.
        —Michael Nichols, Ph.D

Your self-concept and personal identity is seeded and growing long before you are even aware this is happening. If you are treated during childhood with consideration and respect, you will most likely develop confidence and trust in yourself. You will develop a *healthy* sense of guilt. You will feel a moral responsibility to yourself and others, acting with kindness and compassion. If you are abused, humiliated or shamed, your self-image, self-esteem, and sense of confidence will suffer significantly.

Clinical research has shown that children who endure chronic verbal abuse suffer psychological damage that can impair healthy emotional development. They are likely to develop a *toxic* form of shame and guilt, which will plague them for a lifetime. In his book, *Healing The Shame That Binds You*, author and lecturer John Bradshaw emphasizes the negative impact of toxic shame and guilt. He reveals how important it is for children to learn to express needs, feelings and emotions in a healthy manner. If they are shamed by their caregivers for doing so, they are likely to disown these feelings and force them into the unconscious. When enough of their natural drives, feelings and needs are disowned, they begin to feel "wrong" for just being who they are—the seeds of toxic shame have been planted.

As children, by nature, we are curious. We want to explore our environment; we want to learn; we want to grow. We are also, by nature, *creative*. We take things apart, put them back together and take them apart again. We also need to assert our independence, develop our will, and discover our own personal identity. These natural tendencies are part of our "quest," our journey of awakening. They are *critical* to the development of a posi-

tive self-image. These behaviors, however, may be disturbing to our "first lovers," "mummy n' daddy," who may not understand or approve of our inquisitive behavior. Rather than being told why our behavior is not OK with them, oftentimes we are labeled with hurtful words: "bad boy/girl," "stupid," "you're no good," "shame on you."

Toxic Shame and guilt can create a conflict between your natural instinct for *emotional bonding* and your need for *autonomy* and *independence*. As a child, you needed acceptance, approval and love but you also needed to separate from your parents, explore your environment and satisfy your curiosity and creative instincts.

The struggle between closeness and separateness can lead to trouble. If you were made to feel wrong for your behavior without understanding why, you might have begun thinking there was something wrong with *you*, and your self-esteem is further eroded. As you grew into adulthood, you may have developed a negative self-image, mistrust your own impulses and become self-abusive. Your toxic shame and guilt would warp your self-image and your behavior. You then develop

your own internalized set of rules, one of which I call the Inverse Golden Rule: "*I now do unto myself what was done unto me!*" This behavior is what I call "acting *in*."

When you become self-abusive, you create a self-perpetuating "shame cycle." Then your current behavior reinforces the very thing you feel guilty about, keeping your negative self-image alive and kicking. This self-reinforcing cycle is difficult to break since it is so deeply entwined with your self-image and self-esteem.

Remember, our unconscious does not differentiate between real or imagined events. We tend to "think" in pictures. We act according to what we think or *imagine* to be true about ourselves and our environment, *regardless* of the facts! Einstein put it this way: "Imagination is more important than intellect…it is the preview to life's upcoming attractions." Our self-image represents the "previews" to our own personal drama; it defines our character and molds our behavior.

The pathological urge to repeat a behavioral pattern over and over again is called *Repetition Compulsion*. It involves the need to continually be reminded of the shame we felt as a child (or infant) for attempting to express normal, healthy, natural impulses that were made wrong. We then behave in ways that reinforce that self-image, keeping us stuck in a self-inflicted cycle of shame and guilt.

7

"Bad Boy"—The Roots of Character Disorders

It is very difficult for people to believe the simple fact that every persecutor was once a victim.
—Alice Miller

We looked at "Acting *in*" in Chapter 6 and saw how a cycle of self-abuse may result from a faulty self-image. We saw how toxic guilt and shame underlie this faulty self-image and is reflected in your behavior. Sometimes your primary defense is to direct your conflicts outward onto *others*. The flip sides of guilt and shame are resentment and hostility. Rather than "acting in," you act *out*.

"Acting out" means that you project your conflict onto others. Your relationships become the stage upon which you act out your own internal dramas. When you do something that feels important to you while at the same time thinking you "shouldn't" have, you are likely to feel guilty. On the other hand, when you *don't* do something that is important to you because you *think* you "shouldn't," you are likely to feel resentful. Toxic shame and guilt are self-abusive, while resentments and hostilities lead to the abuse of others. Clinical research indicates that women who were abused as children are more likely to unconsciously blame themselves and may tend to attract partners who are abusive to them. Men who were abused as children are more likely to become *abusers* as they grow up.

Some individuals are continually in conflict with authority, have difficulty sustaining intimate relationships and generally cannot get along with others. These individuals have wounds that run much deeper than the neurosis associated with normal guilt and shame. Their primary defense is to blame, project and attack others inappropriately when threatened. In these cases, the seeds of a *character disorder* may have taken root.

These individuals may have been neglected or severely abused emotionally and/or physically at a very early age. They were then unable to normally bond with their primary caretakers and never developed a cohesive sense of "self." If they did something "wrong," they didn't receive proper guidance and discipline, nor did they learn healthy boundaries. Instead, they may have been punished, hit, beat up, kicked and otherwise severely abused and humiliated. Rather than being taught why their behavior was unsatisfactory, their character was assassinated and they grew up believing they were the problem, rather than their actions.

Punishment, as opposed to healthy discipline, retards emotional development and destroys the healthy will in a child. It also models pathological behavior, which is then passed on from parent to child.

I am reminded of a story of a man who was training his parrot to say "uncle." He would beat the parrot with a stick while repeating the command, "Say uncle! Say uncle!" The parrot just sat silently, not uttering a sound. After many unsuccessful attempts, he finally threw the parrot back into the cage with all the other birds, exclaiming what a "stupid" parrot it was. The next day, the man looked into the cage

and was shocked to see his "stupid" parrot beating the *other* parrots with a stick, commanding them to "Say uncle! Say uncle!"

Character disorders run rampant in our society. The anti-social, borderline and narcissistic personalities are just a few. We have all heard the joke about the neurotics who build castles in the sky and the psychotics who live in the castles, while the therapist collects the rent. Those with character disorders, on the other hand, don't pay the rent on time, destroy the castle and refuse to leave when evicted. They will never take responsibility for their role in the problem, blame the landlord (therapist), and feel "abused" by anyone who attempts to hold them accountable for their actions. Character disorders live by their own set of rules, one of which I call the Convoluted Golden Rule: *"I now do unto others what was done unto me."*

Individuals with character disorders will project their anger and hostility onto others and end up in a perpetual war with their own "ghosts in the closet." I once led a group consisting of male offenders on parole for everything from drug abuse, to manslaughter, to murder. There was a young man in this group with a long scar down his face from a knife fight that he bragged about winning. He spent most of his adult life in prison. I asked him, "Were you beat up as a kid?" He sat straight up in his chair, looked me squarely in the eyes and responded with conviction: "Yeah, my dad used to beat me, but only when I *deserved* it!"

The Swiss psychoanalyst specializing in childhood trauma, Alice Miller wrote, "I have no doubt that behind every crime a personal tragedy lies." This man's life was a tragedy in the making and he had already passed a life sentence on himself. There was no chance to appeal. The problem was, this man *never* deserved to be beaten. Nobody does. His defiance was simply a convoluted attempt to regain a will that had been shattered long before he ever had a chance to exercise it in a healthy way. And, as Gandhi aptly maintained, "Where there is no love, there is no will." This man never had a chance at developing a cohesive sense of self or healthy coping skills.

8

The Negatively Inflated Ego—
A Case of False Identity

I would rather be wanted by the police than
not be wanted at all
      —Anonymous

In the previous chapters we focused on toxic shame, guilt and character disorders which resulted from growing up in a less than optimal environment. We noted the negative consequences of corporal punishment and how assassinating a child's character impairs their self-image.

Many of us, however, were fortunate enough not to be raised by "lizards." We probably had "reasonably" normal parents and were provided with some degree of emotional support. I emphasize "reasonable" because it is all a matter of degree. We do live on a wounded planet, and there are no "perfect" parents anymore than there are "perfect" people. Developmental psychologists use the term "good-enough" parents to describe those parents who fall into the category of "normal" by everyday common standards.

On the other hand, many of us were *not* fortunate enough to have such "good enough" parents. We saw in the previous chapter how the young man in my group was predisposed to violence and abuse at a very early age. He was beaten, kicked, and humiliated by a father who, like himself, was also severely abused. When domestic violence is a daily occurrence, its victims grow up without developing a healthy self-image or self-esteem.

I spoke earlier of how our context defines our perception and attitude towards life. If we grew up in the rain and never saw the sunshine, we might never know there was a sun. As

we developed and began relating to others outside our immediate environment, a subtle shift occurred in our perception. We developed a filter that now visualizes our life through the images and rules absorbed from our prior conditioning. No longer is our perception defined by our context. Instead, the reverse is true: *Our context is now limited to, and defined by, our perception of reality.* As Anis Nin wrote, "we don't see things as they are, we see things as *we* are."

We now see the world through the distorted images, the subjective experiences, of our earlier conditioning. Worse yet, our *self*-image is equally as distorted. If "bad boy" has been deeply imprinted into our unconscious, we will act in accordance with that imprint (image). As we have already seen, our unconscious does not differentiate between real or imagined input.

In order to keep this distorted image intact, we utilize another defense mechanism, *projective identification*: we act out in ways that get *others* to behave *toward* us in a manner consistent with that distorted image. We will manipulate others to treat us the way we think we "deserve" to be treated. Our behavior, and the behavior of others *toward* us, simply reinforces and strengthens our already depleted sense of identity.

The bulk of our self-image has already been imprinted into our brain, our "cellular memory," through images, long before we even were able to talk. As we slowly developed the skill of language, we eventually began to develop concepts, a mental frame of reference about ourselves and the world in which we live. These concepts, especially our self-concept has a direct influence over how we *feel* about ourselves—our self-esteem. How we feel about ourselves, in turn, determines how we behave toward others, the manner in which we *actualize* the potential imprinted in our self-image. Our behavior now reinforces our self-image, generating a self-perpetuating cycle of false identity. I say "false" identity (our persona) because beneath this identity

lies the Still, Empty, Non-Dual Self, around which all else revolves—and hopefully evolves!

The degree to which your identity is positive or negative is determined primarily by how supportive your early childhood environment was, how well you were loved, cared for and nurtured while growing up. Without a solid foundation of love and emotional bonding, some individuals develop what is known as a "negatively-inflated ego."

A negatively-inflated ego results when our personal identity is wrapped up with our negative self-*image*, and we find "labels" to define our character to give us some kind of meaning and purpose. "I am lazy;" "I am depressed;" "I am an alcoholic," etc., etc.

It's true that I am using labels myself, speaking of "character disorders," "neurotics," and the like. We need labels to describe our world; all words *are* labels. Words are *symbols*, words are *descriptive*; words *represent* something other than the thing itself. The word "dog" is a symbol, a label, but it is not the dog itself. The problem is that labels can wreak havoc on our self-image when we forget that labels are merely *descriptive*, not *causative*. If we confuse the effect with the cause, or the symbol with the experience, we remain shackled to the shadows of Plato's cave.

Rather than "I am lazy," maybe the truth is I don't enjoy what I am doing. Rather than "I am depressed," maybe I have not learned how to get my needs met in life. Rather than "I am an alcoholic," maybe I have problems that alcohol prevents

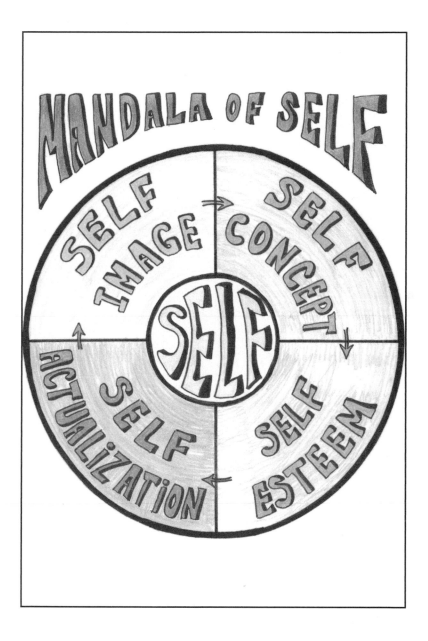

me from facing. Do I drink because "I am an alcoholic? or "am I an alcoholic because I drink?" This question involves far more than splitting hairs. If we can get beneath the labels, we may be able to address the underlying reason, the *experience* that led to the behavior in the first place.

I remember someone jokingly describing a friend of his as a "successful alcoholic" (His friend "successfully" stopped drinking twelve times in less than a year!) This is not meant to trivialize anyone's attempt to straighten out their life and find peace of mind. Using "name tags" or labels to help us identify and confront our problems may be the first step. At some point, however, it may become necessary to go beneath the labels and confront the underlying question, "Who *am* I, really? We will then have to face the issues that plague us and commit to working them through. If we don't, they will linger in our consciousness and perpetuate our suffering until we decide to deal with them.

9

Normal Neurosis:
Issues of Attachment

Why did the flower fade?
I clutched it with my heart in excess of feelings and crushed it.
Why did the lamp go out?
I shielded it with my cloak and it got no air.
　　　　　—Tagore

In the previous chapter, we covered how early childhood abuse can impair our self-image and personal identity. We saw how, without "good enough" parents, life can easily go awry and negatively impact our behavior and the way we approach the world. We also pointed out that many of us were fortunate enough to have been raised in a "reasonably" normal environment. Yet, the line between "normal" and "abnormal" is often a thin one. Regardless, at some point we all seem to come face-to-face with the challenge of trying to make some sense of our lives.

It was Freud, I believe, who said, "It is not the *action*, but the *degree* of the action that differentiates the normal from the neurotic." It is debatable as to whether the terms "normal" and "neurotic" are mutually exclusive or whether they are in fact one and the same. It makes more sense to distinguish between "normal" and "pathological," since the word "pathological" is suggestive of a more extreme version of disease, sickness and suffering. Rather than separating "normal" from "neurotic," I propose fusing them into a hybrid called "normal neurosis." This definition more accurately reflects the garden-variety struggles most of us face on our paths to awakening.

As part of the mainstream population, most of us are able to manage our lives with some degree of "normalcy." We are not plagued with the pathological behaviors of character disorders, nor are we steeped in the conflicts that accompany toxic guilt and shame. Regardless, many of us are still haunted by feelings of insecurity, lack of confidence or self-doubt. And all of us must deal with the stressors associated with daily living such as relationships, career, finances, and the like.

We are all concerned with cultivating health, well being, and peace of mind. We search for ways to feel safe, secure and loved in an insecure and troubled world. How to find peace of mind has been contemplated and debated by scholars, philosophers and mystics throughout history. This may very well be the most daunting challenge we ever face as human beings. It is a challenge that seems to be universal as well as perennial.

"Things"

In a world fraught with change, uncertainty and loss, it is easy to seek security and permanence through attachments and possessions. If you have lost touch with your True Identity, you may seek solace in the world of "things" ("reality," remember?) These objects you thought would bring happiness often end up generating even greater misery and heartache.

Possessions can become burdens, weights you carry around on your shoulders. The world of "things" requires continual maintenance and upkeep. Things demand your time, money and attention. You need to wash them, polish them and keep them clean to forestall their decay. Yet, decay is inevitable. Such is the nature of "reality" (things).

"Situations"

In many situations, it may simply be your attitude about reality that gets in your way. As the German philosopher

Husserl noted, "Perception is intentional." You may be fighting against what simply *is*. Rather than living with "what is," you immerse yourself in an imaginary world of "what if." You transport yourself into an idyllic world where life unhaltingly complies with your demands and expectations. And life, of course, simply doesn't care about your demands. There are many situations in life that you cannot change and must simply accept just the way they are.

Impatience means not "being-here-now" with what is. Impatience takes you away from your senses and into your head, causing greater turmoil, stress and anxiety. The dilemma you must face is "to be here-now or not to be here-now." And when you are not here-now, you end up sabotaging your own efforts to find an acceptable solution to the problem at hand. By resisting the moment, you fall further into the depths of frustration and disappointment.

I often tell my clients, if you want to check your level of emotional development, take an afternoon and stand in line at your local DMV office. By the time you get to the clerk at the window, if you are able to smile genuinely and ask her how her day is going, you are probably an enlightened being! If you weren't enlightened when you got in line, you certainly had an opportunity to attain it while moving slowly toward the front. Or you could have fallen into anger, or shut down into boredom because you were unable to remain absolutely in the moment. Standing in line anywhere can be a catalyst for human development and self-knowledge.

Joseph Campbell said, "The mystic swims in the same water in which the psychotic drowns." We are *all* in the same water! Zen Master D.T. Suzuki once wrote, "Life is like getting into a boat that is just about to sail out to sea and sink." So, if we aren't in the "same water (yet!)," at least we are all in the same boat! Our challenge then is not to go down with the ship, and our lifeboat may just be our attitude.

Relationships

Relationships can be catalysts for personal growth and healing. The Sanskrit word, *yoga*, means "to unite." An intimate relationship is one of the most powerful forms of yoga you can experience. It can serve as a perfect mirror, reflecting back to you your own "shadow," your disowned parts. If you ever want feedback regarding your strengths as well as your weaknesses, just ask your partner—they'll point them out to you without hesitation! In the beginning of a relationship, it seems as though we only see our similarities. After awhile we begin to see our differences. Wouldn't it be nice if we could just see one another?

We already spoke of Plato's mythic "split-aparts," victims of the wrathful god, Zeus, leaving us desperately seeking our "lost selves." That story evokes powerful images of the ultimate experience of "separation anxiety," the loss of our beloved sense of "wholeness." If, however, you mistake the *mirror* for the image *reflected in* the mirror, you can further lose touch with yourself. When this happens, it is easy to project your value and worth onto your partner's acceptance and approval of you. When this happens, you become dependent on the mirror, the relationship, for your sense of well being and happiness. Instead of being a source of healing, the relationship then becomes a source of further pain and suffering.

Loving relationships require an intricate balance between *intimacy* and *autonomy*. You need to be close, intimate and vulnerable with your partner while simultaneously maintaining your own personal integrity, individuality and identity. This would be frightening if you had never developed healthy boundaries as a child. It would be hard enough getting in touch with your own needs, let alone the needs of your partner. Paraphrasing workshop facilitator and author, Stewart Emery: In a healthy relationship we say, "I will stick with you forever." In an unhealthy relationship we say, "I am stuck with you forever."

Fully grasping the mystery of an intimate relationship requires a deep commitment to the emotional health and well-being of one another. If you are up to the task, a relationship can be deeply enriching and empowering. If you are committed to working through your insecurities and fears; if you confront your demand that your partner give you undivided attention; if you acknowledge your partner's needs as well as your own; you may be on the right track. I once read, "The path of wisdom is a long and crooked path, often starting with a broken heart." The source of your struggle, so often, serves as the catalyst in opening your eyes and awakening you to your true identity. Relationships can help you see and feel your true self—what a blessing.

ur environment has a tremendous influence over our beliefs and values. It provides an ironclad template prescribing for us what we must think and how we should be in order to find happiness. This template has been etched into the fabric of our culture since the beginning of time; it is a powerful force and slow to change. It dictates to us the standards by which we measure our self-worth and personal value. If you don't live up to these standards it is easy to misjudge yourself and think there is something wrong with you. Or, on the other hand, if you accept these standards without question, you can further compromise yourself in the pursuit of love and social approval.

When you compromise your values for the sake of approval, you end up creating the very thing you are trying to avoid—accentuated feelings of loneliness and despair. You compare yourself to the "acceptable" standards by which you measure your worth, how you "should" be in order to be loved. When you become attached to how you "should" be, you forget who you "really" are. And then, no matter how hard you try—how thin, how fat, how tall, how short, how well dressed, how well versed—no matter what you do, you never seem to become the "fairest of them all."

You cannot become the "fairest of them all;" You already gave up your natural state of "fairness" within by measuring this state against some external standard that you cannot live up to. When you compare, you lose. Vanity kills. It kills your spirit and deadens your hope, leaving you empty inside. You don't become the "fairest of them all." Rather, you become anorexic—or bulimic—or depressed—maybe even suicidal.

We can travel the world to find the beautiful but if we don't find it within ourselves, we find it not.
— Ralph Waldo Emerson

"Big Boys Don't Cry"

"Big boys don't cry." In this era of so-called enlightened, post-sexist gender roles, that admonition sounds
absurd, doesn't it? Yet I recently had a client whose childhood hero was the tough-guy actor, John Wayne. John
Wayne was his major role model, his idol, who he always
imitated in childhood play. But the line between "play"
and real life became painfully thin. His parents called
him "Little Johnny" as a nickname. Whenever this boy
was upset and started to cry, his dad admonished him by
telling him "Little Johnny doesn't cry." This seemingly
innocuous command had profound and lasting effects.
"Little Johnny" still has difficulty accessing his feelings
or expressing his needs, a difficulty that has cost him
more than one relationship as an adult.

Regardless of the advent of the men's and women's
movements it is easy to assume that these cultural scripts
no longer exist. But centuries of "collective conditioning" do not dissolve in a single generation. This conditioning has penetrated deeply into the fabric of our
consciousness and sometimes overrides our conscious
intention. From an evolutionary perspective, our primitive ancestors were out in the wild battling against
potential threats to their survival and the survival of their
species. "To be killed or not to be killed," was the issue
they confronted daily.

This dilemma haunts 21st century men as well. I have
known Vietnam veterans who described how many of their
closest friends were killed right before their eyes. They
watched helplessly and they could not "feel." If they paused
for just that one moment to lament their loss, their *own* life
was at risk.

I vividly remember a troubled vet who participated
in a co-ed workshop I attended. He told us how his
wounds could not be healed in a "man's world." He could

not simply "will" himself to cry and open up his heart. He told us how he needed the tenderness, the gentleness and the soft touch of his feminine counterpart to open him up to the world of feelings once again. He had to *ask* for assistance, and being "a man," that was hard enough. That's why he was taking the workshop. He needed to confront his fear of vulnerability and grieve his losses.

From a cultural perspective, as we saw from "Little Johnny," the threat of staying in touch with our feelings continues to this day. The threat may not represent "life or death" as it did to our primitive ancestors. Instead, it places the male ego in a vulnerable position. Many of us men have assumed the image of "Rambo," who grits his teeth and magically transcends pain. Otherwise we may face humiliation, ridicule and even contempt if we bare our hearts before our peers. Whether on the playground at school, or around the fathers of all the "Little Johnnys" in our life, the risk is the same. It is never "safe" to feel pain, emotionally or physically. As a defense against ridicule and shame, it is easy to buy into the fantasy that we can transcend any and all pain.

In his book *Emotional Intelligence*, Daniel Goleman refers to the term *alexithymia*, a word coined by a Harvard Psychiatrist, Dr. Peter Sifneos. It is derived from the Greek words *a* ("lack"), *lexi* ("word") and *thymos* ("emotions"). It literally means "without a word for emotions, or feelings." This term does not refer to lack of feelings per se.

Instead, it addresses a problem many people seem to struggle with—the inability to identify or describe what they are feeling in the first place. In my clinical experience, it appears to be more common among men than women.

I have watched many couples in therapy reach a heated impasse because the man won't say what he is feeling during the session. In fact, I've seen more than one man exclaim that he "doesn't *know* what he is feeling." In that very moment—even when he obviously is feeling helpless, frustrated and angry because he is being confronted—he may be right. He may have no idea what he is feeling. That is not an excuse, it is a fact.

Non-attachment

Many adults in the U.S. seem to have difficulty developing strong emotional bonds or maintaining long-term, healthy relationships. The nearly 60% divorce rate is a clear indication of this problem. It also reflects the high value our culture places on independence and autonomy. Independence coupled with the capacity to sustain intimate relationships is a healthy quality, characteristic of an integrated personality. The problem occurs when independence becomes a defense *against* intimacy and emotional bonding. It is simply a matter of intention, conscious or otherwise.

For example, there are pathologically disturbed individuals diagnosed with a Schizoid Personality Disorder. Those who fall into this category were probably severely neglected or abandoned at an early age. Their affect is cold, flat and detached. They isolate themselves from social and personal relationships, preferring solitary activities. They would have no close friends, avoid intimacy at all costs and lack empathy and compassion for others.

The Unabomber showed many of the characteristics of the Schizoid Personality Disorder. No doubt he had many other problems, but his extreme isolation and lack of empathy for others is characteristic of this disorder. It reflects an extremely defensive posture, not characteristic of the mainstream population—a grim reminder of how important emotional bonding is in the development of a healthy sense of self.

More common in our society are those individuals who strive for self-reliance, and decided early in life it wasn't safe to have needs at all. They drive around the neighborhood for hours before daring to ask for directions to avoid looking helpless, needy or inadequate. They never appear to need anything from anybody. If they did, it would threaten the fabric of their defenses. They avoid feeling "attached" to anything—or anyone. Ironically, though, they remain shackled in the worst way. They are utterly attached to never being attached, yet unable to recognize it anymore than a fish recognizes it is swimming in water.

Other individuals may renounce the comforts of mainstream society altogether by retreating inward. They alter their lifestyle, restrict their diet and devote their daily activity to meditation and contemplation. They are committed to discovering truth at all costs. They may attempt to transcend the notion of "attachment" all together, standing strong against all of the temporal delights of the physical world. Some may even successfully accomplish their mission.

These rare enlightened beings radiate the power of love that comes from the depth of their soul. They usually remain humble and reclusive, not as a defense, but simply because they have found an *inner* sanctuary of peace, harmony and balance. They may become great teachers, but there are no strings attached, nor is there any hidden agenda. They don't need to package their wisdom and sell it as a commodity on the open market. Others will seek them out, as they will be attracted to the power of their love like a moth to the light.

I once heard a story of a man seeking Truth. He ventured far into the wilderness of the Himalayas in search of a great master who was said to be enlightened. When he finally reached his dwelling, the seeker was welcomed with a smile. Upon entering, the visitor saw nothing but a sacred scripture, a candle burning, and a meditation mat, upon which the master sat. Stunned, the seeker exclaimed, "Where are all of your things?" The master looked at him with compassion and responded, "Where are all of *your* things?" Without hesitation, the visitor retorted, "Well, I am just passing through." The master gently smiled and said, "So am I, so am I."

There are also those Narcissistic Personality Disorders and Sociopaths who claim to be enlightened, but have another agenda. Rather than remain humble and recluse, these individuals become self-styled "gurus." They venture out into the world, parading themselves as "spiritual teachers" who have come to spread their wisdom. However, their egos soon become enamored of their own inflated self-image and public persona. Rather than spreading their wisdom they spread their "seed" (in the name of God, of course!). Their love is downgraded into lust as they exploit their devotees to gratify their own personal needs and desires.

These individuals have not *really* transcended their desires. Instead, their desires have been forced into their unconscious where they percolate beneath the threshold of awareness. These leaders twist the power of love into the love of power and take advantage of their followers without remorse or concern. Some of these "gurus" have amassed great fortune at the expense of their followers, and many have been under investigation for fraud, smuggling drugs, sexual abuse, and other illegal activities. However, their seductive persuasion, as well as their devotees' misguided hunger for identity and meaning, often camouflages these warnings.

These "gurus" are masters at altering the truth to meet their needs and justify their actions. There is a story of a

guru instructing his students on the importance of staying absolutely present and absorbed in the moment at all times. He said, "When I eat, I eat 100%. When I rest, I rest 100%. When I read, I read 100%."

The next morning one of his students saw him sitting in the cafeteria eating his breakfast and reading the morning paper. The student challenged him: "Sir, I thought you said 'When you read, you read 100% and when you eat, you eat 100%.' But I see now you are reading the paper *while* you are eating. Could you please explain?" The guru quickly retorted, "When I eat *and* read the paper, I eat and read the paper 100%!"

The word "guru" in street language means "Gee, you are you" (and I am me)! In Sanskrit it literally means "dispeller" (*ru*) of darkness" (*gu*). But we don't need to go anywhere to find peace; we must simply look within. Only then will we begin to peel away the layers of defense, insecurity and fear that keeps us tethered to the wall of Plato's cave. In the process, we discover that every experience in life has something to teach us, if we are open to learn from it. Anything that awakens us from the darkness of fear and doubt can serve as our guru.

I am not suggesting we can't learn from others. We can all gain a great deal from the wisdom and experience of others. It can be tremendously valuable to have a mentor, counselor or teacher to assist us in time of need. Problems occur when we begin confusing the teacher with the teachings, or the menu with the meal. If we worship the menu, we'll starve to death no matter how well we memorize the words. The word "education" is from the Latin word, *educere*, to "bring out." Education is not someone telling us what to believe or how to behave. True teachers assist us in discovering and bringing out the truth that already resides within us.

In the previous pages, we explored some unhealthy attachments that hinder growth and stifle peace of mind.

Unhealthy attachments can suck the marrow from our bones—the amount of upkeep and maintenance required to sustain them will drain us psychologically and physically. With unhealthy attachments, we aren't able to appreciate what we have because our energy is so tightly bound to fear, insecurity and self-doubt. If our self-image is defined by these attachments, the cost is even greater because we may depend on them to bolster our ego and give meaning to our lives. Without them, our identity would be threatened.

It is hard to find a neurotic symptom or human vice that
cannot be traced to the desire to possess or the fear of loss.
> —Arthur Deikman, M.D.
> Harvard Psychiatrist and Neurologist

So, "To be attached or *not* to be attached" is the question we must now address. And if we *do* have attachments, is it possible to maintain them in a healthy manner? Can we have attachments without criticizing ourselves for having them—without becoming attached to the fact that we are attached? The question seems to be, at what point can we just let go?

If we choose to eliminate some of our attachments, how can we accomplish this without forcing our desires into the unconscious, as did the fallen guru? How can we become less encumbered and simplify our lives without feeling deprived?

Answering the above questions requires that we pay attention to our *intention* toward these attachments. The attachments themselves are not the primary problem, it is our attitude toward them, and the demands we place upon these attachments—to clear up our lives and bring us peace and happiness—that causes problems. Buddha warned us that the root of our suffering was our grasping and clinging to the transient forms of the world. If we expect the universe to comply with our demands and desires, we inevitably feel disillusioned or let down when these demands remain unmet. The nature of the world we live in is transition and change.

We know that there are secure and insecure attachments at work in human relationships. With healthy attachments, we are capable of surrendering to love. With healthy attachments, we can experience the joy and excitement that comes with opening our hearts to the mystery and intrigue of a relationship. This, I believe, applies to *all* attachments—whether to people or things. Healthy attachments free our energy to fully appreciate and care for what we have because fear or insecurity does not bind us.

Sometimes it is necessary to go after what we *think* we want in order to discover we don't need it. Unless we know *in our own hearts* what we should or shouldn't do, the opinions of others are not helpful. There are things we just *have* to experience along our path in order to move on. Living our life to the fullest means allowing these experiences to penetrate us deeply, to reach into the core of our being. This means trusting our hearts and allowing ourselves to surrender to the spirit of the moment, painful, joyful or neutral, knowing full well that "this too, shall pass." *All* things do. In the meantime, we can have a beautiful time!

If we are unable to experience life fully, we remain suspended between the lure of attachment and non-attachment. We relegate unfulfilled desires to our unconscious, where they "happen to us by fate" as Carl Jung pointed out. Or we may simply end up living our lives in "poverty consciousness," judging and envying others for possessing the things we deprive ourselves of. How these conflicting motives impact our self-image and self-esteem is the subject of the next chapter.

10

Slaying the Dragon—
The Battle Within

What you resist will persist.
—Anonymous

So often, we find ourselves facing conflicting motives in life, which pulls us in opposite directions. Our motives are not always conscious, yet we still feel this internal push and pull. I call this conflict "intention—counter intention."

Maybe your conflict is as immediate as fighting off the urge to stuff down the high calorie foods that you know are "bad" for you. In this dire situation, the dilemma you face is "to eat or *not* to eat"—a common struggle in America today. You may try to deal with this by sheer force of will, in a futile attempt to wrestle all of your desires into submission.

As many of us know from personal experience this approach doesn't generally work. The effort expended in successfully resisting temptation is often exhausting. Then, when our guard is down, we are suddenly ravished by the impulse to reach out and indulge.

What you resist will persist. Not only does temptation persist, our desires increase in intensity proportionate to the degree of our resistance. "For every action there is an equal and opposite reaction." This simple rule of physics seems to apply as much to eating habits as it does to gravitational forces.

We often deal with temptation by force of will, attempting to "slay the dragon" within and force it into submission. This approach works for martial artists in the movies, but generally fails in the real world. Every attack is met with a counter attack, increasing the tension between opposing forces (remember the world of duality). The dragon is bigger than you are from the start, and the more you fight it, the bigger it gets.

The dynamics of other conflicting motives are more subtle, though they are equally potent and all-pervasive in our lives. For example, you might remain in a relationship that you know is unhealthy. Or you may be unhappy in your career, but put no effort into seeking healthy alternatives. You may see that you have a problem, but lack the incentive to resolve it. You may consciously intend to do something, but a counter-intention is operating below the threshold of your awareness, keeping you stuck.

Counter-intentions are closely intertwined with your self-image, self-esteem and personal identity. They reflect your unconscious beliefs and attitude about yourself, and how you perceive reality. They also reflect to you the way you might sabotage your own success. I have worked with many clients who were (consciously) highly motivated, but who (unconsciously) shot themselves in the foot and undermined their own efforts towards success.

You may have high aspirations to accomplish certain goals, but never follow through to completion. You may have dreams that are important to you, but never seem to have the time or energy to realize these dreams. If you don't feel you "deserve" these things, if you don't think you are "smart enough," "good enough," "competent enough," then no matter how strongly you intend toward something, you will also counter-intend with an equal and opposite force.

Since these counter-intentions are unconscious, you can easily rationalize your behavior and invent "reasons" for not following through. You are "too tired," "too busy," "too late;" you don't have the time, the money, the resources, etc., etc. As with hypnosis, *images* evoked in your unconscious directly influence and shape your perceptions of reality. As though acting on post-hypnotic suggestions, you actually believe these rational-lies. You act accordingly, which further reinforces your belief in these imaginary limitations.

There is a direct connection between what you tell your-self and how you act; "where the mind goes, the body is soon to follow." This "self-talk" is generated by the cortex and is a byproduct of your self-image. Your cortex directly influences your hypothalamus, which activates your nervous system and prepares the body for action. Your body, in turn, ignites the limbic system, triggering your feelings.

Since the unconscious does not distinguish between what is real and what is imagined, you act according to what you *imagine* to be true about yourself and the world in which you live. Your *self*-image is a critical determinant of your unconscious bodily responses, your stress level, your posture, and your behavior. The reverse is equally as true. What the body does directly influences how you think and feel, which in turn, reinforces your already established self-image. This reciprocal process generates a self-perpetuating feedback loop between the mind and body. It will automatically replay until you do something to alter its direction. What you can do to break this cycle is the subject of Part Three. But first we will look at what can happen if you *don't* change how you think and feel.

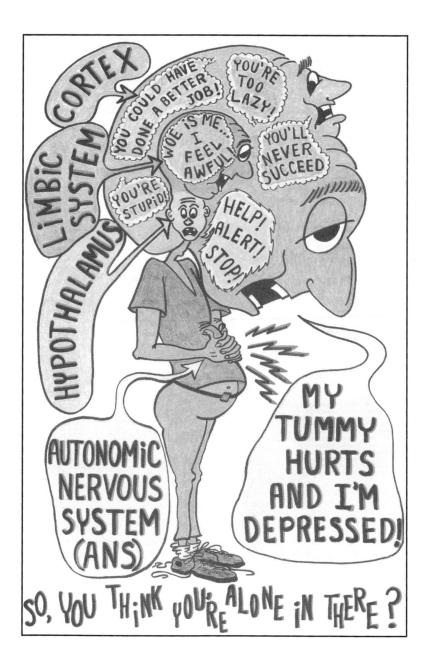

11
Learned Helplessness—
The Roots of Depression

One's real life is often the life one does not lead.
—Oscar Wilde

When you slip into the self-defeating mind/body cycle just described, you are basically conditioning yourself to become helpless. You are training the body to "believe" the mind, and visa versa. Before long, you begin to feel as though you really *don't* have any control over your circumstances. You begin to feel physically and emotionally exhausted, the victimizing dragon appears larger and larger, and you give up. You feel defeated.

Defeat and helplessness are the underpinnings of depression. Depression is epidemic in today's world. Depression drains your energy and leaves you immobilized, feeling helpless and afraid. Everyday life seems out of your control and your depression deepens. You look for anything to numb your pain, to lift your spirits to get you through the day. The activities and things you turn to for relief end up producing the opposite effect, leaving you more depressed.

LEARNED HELPLESNESS:

DEPRESSION IS BOTH THE CAUSE AND CONSEQUENCE OF NEGATIVE THOUGHTS

Your behavior now reinforces the very thing you are trying to avoid—your pain and the accompanying feelings of helplessness. Your actions increase your depression, generating a truly vicious cycle of learned helplessness. Your self-defeating behavior becomes both the cause and the consequence of your depression. If you doubt your ability to perform well at a certain task, you will not do as well as you think you "should" and consequently you will feel more depressed and helpless. This is a lose-lose situation. You are on a downward spiral. Not only do you lose the round, you lose the fight altogether. The dragon wins again and gets stronger and bigger.

Once you give up the sense of control or power over your life, you can easily lose hope. Without hope, there is nothing to strive for. Hope is the capacity to see beyond your immediate situation, to see possibilities for the future. Without hope for the future, there is no sense "reviewing your past" or "living in the present." Without hope, you resign yourself to your self-induced fate. You are on a psychological death march.

This slow psychological death is not uncommon when your search for meaning and identity has been thwarted. Without realizing it, you gradually adjust to unfavorable conditions while further losing touch with who you "really" are. You try harder and harder but fail to "fit in". You develop maladaptive behaviors to cope with life on a wounded planet.

Abraham Maslow, the late humanistic psychologist, called this "psychopathology of the average so widespread and undramatic we don't even know it is happening." We have become addicted to TV, alcohol, drugs (legal and illegal), food, work, sex, or anything else that seems to soothe our pain. Or, as Thoreau points out, we end up living life in "quiet desperation."

Measuring your worth by cultural standards never serves you well. You don't live in a "one size fits all" world so you end up feeling more disillusioned and let down. Consensus reality is nothing more than a collective hallucination. If you buy into the cultural prescriptions for sanity and health, these can include prescriptions for *more* drugs to numb you from your pain!

Most of us have probably heard about the "frog in the pot." If you drop a frog into a pot of boiling water, it will jump out immediately. But if you drop a frog into a pot of lukewarm water, it will swim there and quietly adjust to its environment.

Then, if you slowly turn the heat up, the frog will readjust to the warmer temperature. It remains comfortable and seemingly content. If you keep turning up the heat gradually, the frog will continue to adapt to its changing environment—until it eventually dies before the water starts to boil.

By the way, I didn't perform this experiment myself, though legend has it that it was executed (no pun intended)

at a major university. No one has attempted this experiment literally on human beings, though I suspect the outcome might be the same. This provides a brutal but important metaphor for the human struggle for meaning and identity in a world gone slightly mad.

I shared this "frog" metaphor with a client whose relationship was falling apart because he was not willing to give up his daily addiction to smoking marijuana. He immediately quipped, "I think I am a frog *on* pot!" No further comment was necessary. Whether *on* pot or *in* the pot, the end result was similar.

If you have not lost all hope, I want to remind you of the first law of holes: "If you're not in one, stop digging!" Otherwise the hole gets deeper and deeper. Before long you have dug your way into Plato's cave and are peering at shadows in front of you. If you are in over your head, you may need to implement the second law of holes: "If you're in one, look up, not down!" And when you look up from Plato's cave, you will be surprised to see the light shining above.

If you muster the courage, you can rise upward and rediscover the brilliance from which you descended. You can "remember" what you already knew before the veil of forgetfulness fell upon your consciousness. With renewed hope you can venture onto the path of healing. There you will not only heal your own wounds, but also contribute to healing our planet as a whole. This is the subject of Part Three.

PART THREE
Self-Aceeptance—
The Heart of Healing

To the degree that we have compassion for ourselves,
we will have compassion for others. Having compassion
starts and ends with having compassion for all those
unwanted parts of ourselves, all those imperfections that
we don't even want to look at.
> —Pema Chodron
> American-born Buddhist nun and teacher

12

Attitude of Awakening—
Awareness, Acceptance, Action

"I am *Awake*"
    —Buddha

Self-awareness is the beginning of healing. Healing begins when we are able to step back and look at ourselves, to acknowledge our wounds. The noted author Daniel Goleman refers to self-awareness as "the keystone of emotional intelligence." Fritz Perls, the late German born psychiatrist and founder of Gestalt Therapy, suggested that "awareness, itself, is curative." Simply by noticing, paying attention and focusing on a particular issue, change will naturally happen. Eastern teachings refer to this process as *witnessing* or exercising the objective observer inside of you.

One way we actually *block* self-awareness is by *judging* ourselves harshly. I have worked with many people over the years who, as soon as they see something they don't like about themselves, start putting themselves down. (See the cartoon in chapter six, you'll know which one.) When we start a negative internal monologue and become overly self-critical, we are no longer able to objectively observe ourselves or others.

In my clinical experience, self-awareness is essential for personal growth, but by itself, it is *not* enough. Carl Rogers, the late humanistic psychologist, spoke of *unconditional positive regard* as being critical to the healing process. Eastern traditions refer to witnessing *without judgment* as being essential to the path to enlightenment. Unconditional positive regard simply means loving and accepting yourself for who you are in the moment, because that *is* who you are (whether you like it or not.) When you harshly judge yourself, you actually strengthen the grip of the negative behavior that you dislike. You can't change anything until you first accept it—as it is. Psychologists refer to this as the paradoxical theory of change. Remember, "what you resist will persist."

Many people misconstrue the notion of self-acceptance to mean that whatever they do is "OK" because "that's just the way they are." This attitude embodies new-age narcissism. There is a big difference between "acceptance" and "approval." Accepting something you have done doesn't mean you necessarily approve or condone the action. It simply means acknowledging the truth of what you've done—whether you like it or not! And if you aren't able to accept what is true in the moment, you are helpless to do anything about it. You can never be what you are not. By accepting "what is," you allow room for greater awareness to arise. To begin to heal, you must first recognize and accept the truth of your situation—because it is what it is.

I once worked with a young couple whose relationship was in jeopardy because the husband broke their vow of monogamy. Agonizing over that, he kept saying, "I just don't understand what got into me. It just wasn't *me!*" I asked, "Who *was* it then, if it *wasn't you?*"

There was a deep silence. The question penetrated beneath the surface of his monologue, revealing an essential message of his adultery: "It *was* me, and if I don't lift the veil of denial, I will never discover the disowned shadow that lurks beneath my awareness, grabbing hold of me when my guard is down."

What we don't handle consciously is relegated
to the unconscious and happens to us by fate.
               —Carl Jung

Rather than beat your own personal dragon (yourself) into submission, you must approach the dragon with kindness and compassion. Embrace the dragon by establishing a relationship with it. Learn about its weaknesses and vulnerabilities. Like a martial artist, you must absorb and flow with the energy of the opposing force in order to subdue it. This is done without resistance or aggression.

Once you have befriended your shadow, you will begin to recognize it as a vital source of your creativity and power. What once lurked beneath the threshold of your awareness is now exposed to the light of consciousness. Through self-acceptance you expand your awareness. Yet awareness and acceptance are only part of the healing process. Self-awareness and acceptance often facilitate a release of energy that has long been repressed—this energy must now be directed into creative outlets. What is now required is a commitment to positive action and the determination to follow through.

On the road to healing, awareness without positive action is like a bird with clipped wings. It can flutter around but never get anywhere. Many "awareness junkies" today learn the language of healing but continue to act in ways destructive to themselves and others. Their motto is, "That's just the way I am!" Their limited recycled awareness actually serves as a defense *against* penetrating further into the heart of the problem, where healing begins. "Just the way I am" actually signifies that I am clinging to false identity and refusing to let go.

The late humanistic psychologist, Abraham Maslow researched highly successful people, those who seem able to accomplish their goals in life. One quality these individuals share is the ability to take positive action. They actively endeavor to reach their fullest potential, which Maslow dubbed *self-actualization*. Self-actualized individuals transform their shadows into creative self-expression. They achieve success by utilizing the energy from previously disowned parts of themselves.

One of the downsides of self-awareness and action is that both can become potential weapons of self-destruction, setting into motion a negative feedback loop that pivots around our self-judgments. For example, you could become aware of some facet of yourself you don't like and judge yourself critically, even though you haven't really *done* anything. You might then *act* in ways destructive to yourself or others. I worked with a young married woman who became increasingly aware of her sexual fantasies toward men outside her marriage. She judged herself severely and was deeply ashamed. She then "acted out" by compulsively overeating. That was her way of "stuffing" her unwanted thoughts and sexual feelings. Once she recognized and got past her self-judgments, she was able to address the unresolved issues in her relationship that led to these fantasies in the first place.

This phenomenon also happens in reverse. We might act in a negative manner toward someone or something and judge ourselves afterward, which then negatively reinforces our false impression that something *is* fundamentally "wrong" with us. The young man who broke his vow of monogamy is a good example of this dynamic. His affair evoked feelings of shame and guilt which needed to be resolved before he could see more deeply into the causes underlying his actions.

The opposite of judgment is acceptance. Self-acceptance is "the heart of healing." It allows us to bypass the negative feedback loop, which keeps us tethered to our pain. Self-acceptance is the foundation upon which self-awareness and action rest for their strength and support. It modulates their function and determines how positively or negatively they will influence our lives.

Self-acceptance never means resigning myself to "just the way I am." Self-acceptance means first *acknowledging* where "I am" in a non-defensive manner. I am then in a position to gain greater awareness and clarity into the

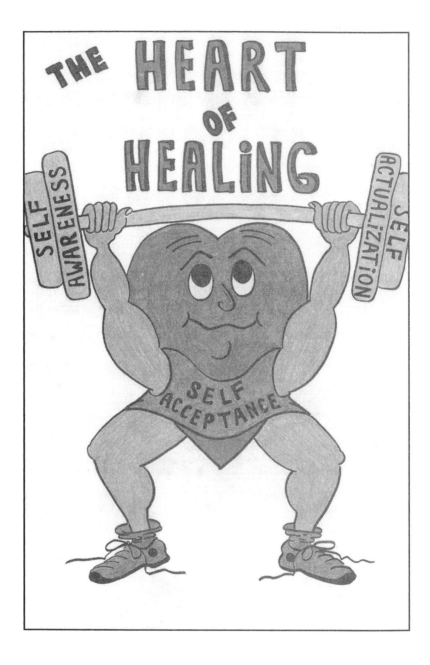

choices I have made that got me where "I am" in the first place.

Awareness, acceptance and action. I refer to the integration of these three qualities as "An Attitude of Awakening." When integrated, awareness, acceptance and action work in concert to promote growth and facilitate personal awakening. The true measure of intelligence is the ability to make your life work. When your actions line up with your deeper intentions, you

are more likely to produce the results you want in life and to find peace of mind.

"AAA" may be the cheapest, yet most effective, psychological insurance there is. You need only invest a little time and energy into developing your emotional and psychological skills, and the returns will last a lifetime. As the "three As" become synchronized within you, the defenses you once depended on for survival slowly begin to dismantle. This liberates you from a self-imposed prison of denial, while simultaneously opening your heart to an even greater capacity for self-awareness and action.

Returning to the couple whose relationship was threatened by the husband's affair: once he stopped trashing himself, he began reflecting on how he got himself into that situation. Only by first accepting what "was," could he expand his awareness and probe more deeply into the underlying dynamics that led him to *act* in a way that "just wasn't him." This man had grown up in a family consumed by sexual repression and secrecy. Now he began to recognize the conflict and shame he carried, and how he had disowned his sexual desires by forcing them into his unconscious. And how his own repressed desire had "happened to him by fate."

By accepting his actions and expanding his awareness, this man was able to consciously integrate his disowned sexuality in a healthy manner. He could then act with a greater awareness of his vulnerabilities without tripping over his unconscious when he wasn't paying attention. Refusing to berate himself allowed him to focus his awareness on making healthy choices in the present. Now he sees, with greater clarity, how conflicts from his past have a subtle but powerful influence over the choices he makes as an adult.

The word "healing" literally means, "to make *whole*." A commonly held misconception about past wounds is that once you acknowledge them, they will somehow just disappear. Your inner conflicts will lessen but they will never disappear. "Wholeness" means you accept the parts of yourself that you previously disowned and *integrate* them into your conscious self. You thereby accept them as part of the greater "whole" of who you are. These conflicts don't *recede*: instead, your awareness *expands*. Your wounds *appear* to recede, proportionately, giving you more opportunities to make *conscious* choices and to be accountable for your actions. This is why the explanation for it is called the *paradoxical* theory of change.

Becoming "whole" takes great courage. You must come face to face with the things you fear the most and embrace them with heart. This can sometimes be painful. Through self-acceptance you are more likely to penetrate to the roots of your conflicts. You may uncover wounds from your past that have never been faced or recognized. You may re-experience losses that you have never grieved, such as the loss of a loved one, or possibly the loss of love you never received as a child. Some of us have been physically, sexually and/or emotionally abused. Some of us were unwanted or emotionally abandoned before we *consciously* knew what was happening.

Loss has many forms and faces. These wounds don't "go away" with time. Instead, they are "relegated to the unconscious." As the renowned medical intuitive and lecturer Caroline Myss wrote, "Our biography becomes our biology." Our past is stored in our emotional memory and continually influences the people we attract and our decisions and actions in the present. They influence our self-esteem, our self-concept, the kinds of relationships we attract, and our attitude toward life in general.

We know that emotional bonding is critical to the healthy development of mammals, especially primates and human beings. If we haven't grieved our losses from the past, the stored, unexpressed pain prevents us from developing healthy bonds in the present. The resulting emotional isolation undermines any hope we may have for the future. This can leave us stuck with negative self-defeating behavior and feelings of helplessness.

Authentic emotional healing is an on-going interrelated sequence of awareness, acceptance and action, a positive spiral that penetrates deeper and deeper into the infinite embrace of our true selves. Grieving is a natural and healthy part of emotional healing, ensuring our further growth and healthy development. How we grieve the past and heal our wounds is the topic of the next chapter.

13

Grieving Our Past— The Three "R's"

*I imagine one of the reasons people cling to their
hate so stubbornly is because, they sense, once the
hate is gone, they will be forced to deal with their pain.*
—James Baldwin

Grieving can take many forms and naturally varies from person to person, depending on the nature and severity of the wound, as well as the psychological hardiness of the individual involved. Nevertheless, all sentient beings experience grief, and in humans the grieving process has natural stages. Given these individual variations, there are still some common steps that go hand in hand with the grieving process. While not wanting to *over*simplify these steps, I will present them here in a simple formula. The steps involved in grieving are *reliving, reworking* and *reframing*—what I call the "Three 'R's" of emotional healing.

Reliving involves revisiting our past. It requires going back to the "original scene" in your mind, recalling the trauma of the wound and remembering the details as succinctly as possible. This can be done through such techniques as guided imagery, role-playing, gestalt, psychodrama or any other form of memory retrieval. These processes activate the unconscious and evoke images that have long been repressed. These emotional memories are the blueprints we unknowingly follow in designing the structure of our lives.

Research in neuropsychology suggests that by reconstructing the past in the present via our *explicit* or conscious memory, we simultaneously activate the *implicit* or unconscious emotional memory associated with the event, as well. In his book, *The Emotional Brain*, Joseph LeDoux Ph.D, calls the point where these two kinds of memory converge the "working memory." Activating the working memory thrusts open the "floodgates" of emotional arousal and the past and present become one.

Reworking involves learning constructive new ways to respond to old wounds. Implicit memory is timeless. It doesn't differentiate between the past and the present. Old wounds remain forever active as unfinished business in our unconscious until we *do* something to change their emotional meaning. As an infant, toddler or young child, we lacked the emotional tools available to us now. By reactivating the past in the present we are in a better position to act *now* in ways we could never have accomplished *then*.

Reworking often involves expressing a full range of emotions that surface during the re-experience. We may feel rage, anger, fear, hurt or sadness, or any combination of emotions. If we have withheld rage, we may need to fight back now, verbally and even physically. We may protest out loud what was (is being) done to us, *demanding* that it stop now. This is called *cellular release*. We are emptying the caldron of emotions that have been stored inside of us for years. Rather than continue beating *ourselves* up (see cartoon, chapter 6) or unconsciously projecting our rage onto others (see cartoon, chapter 7), we can now *symbolically* direct our rage towards the source of our pain. This is done in the supportive context of a therapist's office or in a workshop designed to work in this manner.

I am not suggesting that expressing anger or any other emotion necessarily represents unfinished business from our past. Accessing and expressing our feelings in the present is essential for healthy functioning. If we experience loss, grieving that loss facilitates healing. If we are worried, healthy anxiety heightens our awareness of a potential threat to our safety. If the threat is imminent, or our boundaries are violated, expressing anger can protect us from harm.

Expressing healthy anger and venting old rage are two different matters altogether. Rage is more commonly associated with deeper issues that are *triggered* by the current situation. Some research indicates that venting rage does nothing but intensify the rage already present in the individual. This may be true if venting rage is an end in itself, such as flipping someone off for cutting in front of us on the freeway.

Venting is different from releasing. The missing ingredient would be constructive *intention*. Venting is "recycled" rage that builds momentum each time it is re-experienced. If we don't get beneath the surface of the rage and deal with the original wound, we continue acting it out by projecting it onto others indefinitely.

Releasing rage is another matter. When expressing rage is a means toward a worthy end, when we are working it through in order to get to the source of the pain that underlies the rage, then the expression or re-enactment is productive. This gets us beyond the current event that triggered the emotion. We always need to get to the heart of the matter, the source of the pain, so we can release the grip of our past. This will revitalize our energy and give us hope for the future.

Another step is crucial in permanently anchoring these changes in place. This final stage involves *reframing*. Once you have revisited unresolved past events and worked through the emotional content associated with them, you are in a position to alter your perception of these events. This requires the power of your imagination. We know that the unconscious never differentiates between real or imagined input. Since our implicit, emotional memory is not time-bound, the past and the present are fused together. We re-engage our explicit memory by recalling past events and simultaneously arouse the implicit emotional memory associated with those events. Using guided imagery tools, we can now reframe these events so they evoke a different emotional response.

Reframing also refers to mentally altering your perception of past events by consciously attributing new meaning to them. What you *tell* yourself about the situation in your currently aroused emotional state can actually give a new emotional flavoring to these past events. Through the use of affirmations and cognitive restructuring, you can permanently anchor these meanings into the "working memory" of your brain. Your brain will then make positive associations with old painful events, thereby changing your emotional memory forever. You are not changing your explicit memory of what *actually* happened. Instead, you are changing the *meaning* of the event and therefore your emotional *reaction* to that memory.

Sometimes a trauma may be current and not involve repressed memories at all. The process of dealing with the situation, however, remains the same. The woman whose husband had the affair is a good example. When she found out about the affair, her initial response was shock, numbness and denial. They tried to work it out on their own, but weren't successful. She hadn't yet found a healthy way to deal with her own pain—feelings of resentment and betrayal began to surface. Their relationship reached an impasse and they eventually sought help.

By addressing the issue in therapy, she began reliving the painful details of being told about the affair. This brought up feelings of anger, sadness and hurt that she needed to acknowledge and express. Eventually she was able to alter her perception of the situation. She reframed it in a way that had a different emotional meaning associated with it— his affair no longer meant *she* wasn't good enough. She recognized that her husband really *did* love her and was truly remorseful for what he had done. She acknowledged that she also loved him, and was choosing to work it out. They *both* realized there were problems in their relationship that needed to be addressed, and the affair brought these problems to the surface.

Changing the meaning of past experiences and the emotional memory associated with them inevitably leads to one of the most difficult challenges of the healing process—learning how to forgive. Forgiveness works both ways. You need to forgive yourself, and those whom you feel have hurt you in the past. We will examine forgiveness in the next chapter and see how crucial it is to feeling at peace and experiencing the joy of being alive.

14

Forgiveness—Living
from the Heart

Whatever our religion, we know that
if we really want to love, we must first
learn to forgive before anything else.
　　　　—Mother Teresa

Forgiveness moves in two directions. In chapters six and seven we discussed the negative effects of feeling guilty, becoming overly self-critical and judging ourselves harshly. Or we may feel resentful and project this onto others by holding judgments against them. These are defensive postures that keep us from dealing with the pain that resides beneath the threshold of our awareness. Guilt and resentment are flip sides of the same coin and we may oscillate between the two. Either may be our dominant defense. When we begin experiencing one, the opposite will emerge simultaneously and also need to be processed.

Let's return to the couple whose relationship was threatened because the husband had an affair. Once he began acknowledging the unexpressed guilt and shame he carried with his sexuality, feelings of resentment began to emerge. He then began working through the anger and deep grief he felt toward his parents for contributing to his sexual uncertainty and self-doubt. These were ancient wounds associated with an unavailable, alcoholic father, and a mother who had emotionally smothered him and sexualized their relationship.

He also began to recognize how he was projecting repressed anger toward his parents onto his wife, and then acting this out in the form of an affair. Unfortunately, acting it out actually reinforced his guilt, which had preceded the affair. His self-esteem and sexual identity were impaired and he was trapped in a cycle of pain. His behavior maintained a negative feedback loop that would have continued indefinitely had he not taken steps to change it.

Guilt, as a defense, frequently carries the underlying message that "If I feel badly enough about what I did, I must be a good person after all." Guilt is often a desperate attempt to salvage some sense of value and self-worth. The irony is, we already have value. Our challenge is to acknowledge our worth without punishing ourselves to prove it. Self-inflicted punishment is a common characteristic of those with a negatively-inflated ego (chapter eight)—"The worse I am, the more value I have as a person." Getting beyond the guilt means addressing the self-esteem issues residing beneath the surface. It means confronting the reasons we think we need to suffer to feel worthwhile in the first place.

Once you have grieved your losses, you are in a position to forgive yourself and move on. Self-forgiveness is not limited to our missteps as adults. Most of us carry some guilt and shame over childhood experiences we think and feel were our fault. When parents divorce, children often blame themselves as if something were wrong with them. Victims of sexual abuse also frequently blame themselves. Many were told it *was* their fault by parents or other adults when they revealed the abuse. As adult children of abuse, it is easy to become preoccupied with feelings of disgust and self-loathing. Whether real *or* imagined, self-blame and guilt must be confronted and dealt with so we can let it go once and for all. If we don't forgive ourselves, we remain stuck in perpetual negativity and self-doubt.

Holding resentment toward others also keeps us locked in negativity. Lecturer and author Sam Keen summed it up well: "Resentment is the poison *we* take in the hopes that it will kill the other person." Poison it is. Resentment is toxic

to the body. Emotional wounds remain seething in our limbic system or emotional brain until we consciously examine them. Because the past and the present are not differentiated in this part of the brain, when we obsess over past transgressions, we re-arouse the limbic system, thus reinforcing the memory and feelings from the original event. We need to forgive so you can free up our energy and move on. Otherwise we carry around negative and destructive cellular memory.

The director of the Stanford Forgiveness Project, Fred Luskin, Ph.D, has shown that the way you *think* about past hurts directly influences how well you are able to forgive and heal your past. In his book *Forgive for Good*, Dr. Luskin wrote: "The way we create our story will be of utmost importance." Many people develop what he calls a "grievance story"—"The painful things that you have endured but not healed from." He goes on to say, "At the very core of creating a grievance or grudge is that something happened that we did not want to happen." It is not what happens to you, but the *meaning* you attribute to the event, that keeps you from letting go of and healing your past wounds.

If it has negative elements, our "story" perpetuates our suffering, weakens our immune system and leaves us more vulnerable to sickness and disease. I once heard it said, "We don't suffer from the thoughts that go through our heads, only the ones we hold onto." Holding onto resentment siphons away emotional energy and motivation, and drains our vitality, aliveness and creativity. If we don't confront these toxic thoughts and feelings, we are held captive by our own animosity. Resentment retards our emotional growth, and impedes our ability to develop compassion and empathy for others.

My clients often ask, "Why should I forgive them? They knew what they were doing!" This is an important question. Let me answer by asking, would it have made a difference if they *hadn't* known what they were doing? This is a trick question. As an adult, you may say, "Yes, I could forgive them." Yet the child in you will be hollering "No!" This wounded child is still hurting and needs to have its voice heard. Otherwise, it will never let go of you emotionally, no matter how hard you try to rationalize and be reasonable. Whether or not people knew they were hurting you often causes confusion and creates a conflict between your head and your heart

Once you have gone through the grieving process outlined in the previous chapter, you are ready to move toward the final step of forgiveness. Begin by recreating the situation from your past, as before. This time, however, use the power of your imagination to see the situation and see it now through the eyes of compassion and empathy. This exercise can be difficult, and takes practice. I know it sounds unreasonable to have compassion for someone who has hurt you. It makes little practical sense. But, as Pascal wrote, "The heart has reasons that reason knows nothing of." The heart's "reason" is to heal its wounds—to become whole again.

By imagining and seeing the person and/or situation through the eyes of compassion, you are changing your story and sending a different message to your emotional brain. This message echoes down to your hypothalamus. The hypothalamus, in turn, signals your autonomic nervous system that your body can relax, take a deep breath and feel safe. Your body then responds by sending signals *back* up to your emotional brain signaling that it is safe, thus reinforcing the relaxation response. In a literal sense, you are defusing your "fight or flight" response to the situation by *rewiring* the neural pathways in your brain to receive a different message.

As with acceptance, compassion doesn't mean we condone another person's behavior. Nor do we have to "like" the person. Compassion transcends the boundaries of conditional love altogether. By imagining compassion in

difficult situations we are less likely to *personalize* the behavior of others when they hurt us. This doesn't mean we are dismissing our pain prematurely. Instead we can integrate painful experiences by first entering into them and fully acknowledging them. We need to get to the hurt and pain that underlies resentment. We can do this by allowing these feelings to penetrate us to the core. We feel them deeply so we can move on. We can never eliminate past hurts. We can, however, regulate our reaction to them in the present.

This is where your ability to choose comes in, choices you may not have had at the time you were hurt. You can *choose* to see and feel your past from a different vantage point. You might realize that those who hurt you may *not* have known better. You won't personalize their actions; you'll recognize that beneath their animosity they were also afraid, and their fear was rooted in ignorance. Because they themselves were wounded, they may *have* been doing the best they could.

Most people are not lizards in drag. We don't really intend to hurt one another. Very few of us looked down at our innocent newborn infant in its crib and consciously contemplated how we could make that child suffer for life. When we act from ignorance, we *do* hurt others, whether we intended to or not. Jesus said it best: "Forgive them, for they *know not* what they do."

But from the vantage point of forgiveness, whether or not they did "know" is no longer the issue. What matters is what we *tell* ourselves about the situation or person effecting us, and how we hold these feelings inside ourselves. By dissolving the negativity that surrounds our heart, love *naturally* arises within us. As Alice Miller points out, "The sun does not need to be told to shine when the clouds part, it simply shines." When we surrender to this love, it spills over to the hearts of others, because love *is* for-*giving*. Love is where healing begins and ends.

To live your life in this manner requires a daily commitment to liberating yourself from the reins of the past and to creating peace of mind. By continually reinforcing and rehearsing this action of forgiveness, you will slowly replace animosity with a greater capacity to feel compassion and empathy for others. You will then see more clearly the wounded hearts of all those who have hurt you. And by healing the wounds of your own heart, you naturally contribute to healing our wounded planet.

If we could read the secret history of our enemies,
we should find in each person's life sorrow and
suffering enough to disarm all hostility.
        —Henry Wadsworth Longfellow

Transforming your resentments and judgments into compassion is an art that requires dedication. The following daily exercise will assist you in developing this art: Each time you catch yourself judging another person (or yourself), immediately follow that judgment with feelings of empathy and compassion for that person (or yourself). Do this *regardless* of what they (or you) have said or done. If you are going to practice forgiveness, you must take it all the way. If you start making exceptions based upon your own standard of what is forgivable and what is not, it negates the whole forgiveness process.

When you begin this practice, you will find it a lot more difficult than you might expect. If you stick with it, your tendency to judge yourself or others will slowly diminish. Your capacity for empathy and compassion will gradually expand. As you unfetter yourself from the past and learn to forgive, you will find it easier to be present in the moment and move toward the future with greater hope.

15

Being "Here-Now," or "There-Then."

If you don't know where you are going,
You will probably end up somewhere else.
—Laurence J. Peter

Historically, traditional psychology has stressed the importance of our past in influencing our future. It has placed great emphasis on the role our past played in developing our character and determining our fate. Today, the human potential movement emphasizes "living in the present," remaining in the *"here and now."*

Rarely, however, has psychology focused on how important the *future* is in influencing our present. The future is viewed as some kind of abstraction out in front of us, beyond our immediate reach. It is easy to assume that the future is only a byproduct, an outcome, of what we do in the present. The past and the present are important. We know with certainty that what we did yesterday, and what we do today, will influence how tomorrow turns out.

There is more to our life than simply being pushed by our past. Tomorrow is not only an *effect* of yesterday and today. It is also a *cause*. The Greek word, *telos*, means "final cause," or *that toward which you aspire*. Not only are we pushed by our past, and focused in the present, we are also pulled by the future. An acorn is destined to become an oak, not a willow or a pine. There are no other options. The acorn is moving *toward* becoming a mature oak tree, in the future, *regardless* of how well it was cared for in the past.

We are intentional creatures. We are creative beings, and creativity is a dynamic process in perpetual motion and flux. We are always moving toward something, whether we recognize it or not. We don't act randomly; consciously or unconsciously, we act with intention. The key is to act with *conscious* intention in the *present*, so you can see where you are going in the *future*. Wayne Gretzky, the NHL hockey player, said it clearly: "It's not as important to know where the puck is now as to know where it will be." This means you need to have a vision— to know where you'd like your "puck" to be tomorrow. And your vision is fortified from the newfound hope you fostered through integrating your past.

When we sit down, we usually sit to rest or relax. When we eat, we eat to satisfy hunger or gratify our desires. When we exercise, we exercise to strengthen our body and maximize our health. Even when we meditate, to some degree we meditate with intention. We meditate to quiet our thoughts, to be *present* in the moment, to find peace of mind. Each of these actions is movement *toward* something, toward the future. And that future is unfolding through each action we take in the present.

Let's say you are sitting down to study for a midterm exam coming up next week, and a classmate says, "The exam is not until next week. I'm going to stay 'in the now' and party instead." Actually he is no more "in the now" than you, he just has different *intentions* regarding the future. Your intention is to do well on the exam while his is to have fun and party. Neither action is "right or wrong," the difference is simply a matter of choice or priority.

By remaining *conscious* of how you choose your priorities, you are more likely to recognize whether or not your present behavior is truly in alignment with your higher intentions. If your classmate's higher intention was to do well in that class and graduate with highest honors, he could ask himself if "partying" was in

alignment with that intention. Is he consciously moving in the direction of fulfilling his vision, or has he gone astray without realizing it?

The more you have transformed and integrated your past wounds, the better able you are to focus in the present. The more you are focused in the present, the more likely you are to act with conscious intention toward the future. And this future forever calls you toward your destiny; your own *telos*, which seeks to actualize its fullest potential. When your past and future are in alignment with your higher intention, you are living your vision to the fullest in each moment.

16

Living Our Vision Now

Imagination is more important than intellect.
It is the preview to life's upcoming attractions.
—Albert Einstein

Since our unconscious does not distinguish between real or imagined input, if you cannot imagine something, it most likely won't come into being. Your body needs clear directions. "Where the mind goes, the body is soon to follow." The images you hold in your mind, your brain, directly impact the hypothalamus, igniting the body for action.

The power of your imagination represents both the creation and realization of your destiny. With renewed hope, your energy is now available to focus on realizing your vision—to see where your "puck" is going. Rather than rehearsing failure by imaging fear (Fantasy Experienced As Real), you instead imagine success—you "see" yourself *now* as you would like to be in the future—as though it *is* true right now. You are now rehearsing success rather than failure. As George Eliot wrote, "It is never too late to be what we might have been."

Once you have created your vision and rehearsed it in your imagination, you are ready to *act*. Your body is the *vehicle* of creative expression. You need to exercise this vehicle by acting in alignment with your vision. This means taking chances, risking disapproval or failure, and challenging your self-imposed limitations. Action without clear intention is like a runaway train. Worse yet, intention without action is like a train that never left the station.

There is a trait common to *both* self-actualized *and* depressed individuals: they both look *within* when things don't go the way they intended. The telling difference is what they do when they look within. Depressed individuals tend to *blame* themselves, find fault, and criticize themselves. They settle into despair, reinforcing the cycle of learned helplessness. Self-actualized individuals, instead, reflect on what they learned from the situation and look for ways to do better next time.

Your perspective can define the difference between success and failure. Some people faced with opportunities and challenges see only obstacles and hardship. Others, faced with obstacles and hardships, see only opportunities and challenges. It is all a matter of perspective. We spoke earlier of how our perception defines our context. As the singer, Roger Miller poetically said, "Some people walk in the rain, others just get wet."

Self-actualized people never give up. They persevere against all odds. They transform obstacles into challenges,

using every experience as an opportunity to learn and grow. Every new moment offers new challenges. When they fall, they get back up and try again…and again…until they succeed or the situation changes.

There is an old adage, "A philosopher is known by his *words*, a master by his *works*." In actuality, we are *all* known by our works. What you *do* with your life is a clear reflection of who you are in this ever-changing moment. When you act with conscious intention toward realizing your vision, your head and heart come into alignment. When your head and heart are in alignment, you begin to discover the deeper essence of who you *really* are, which takes us to the final chapter.

17

Who Am I, Really?

What we are looking for is what is looking.
—St. Francis

What is your name? You are not defined by your name. It was *given* to you at birth. Your name is how you and others *identify* your body. Yet the cells of your body are continually mutating. In seven years, all the cells of your body have died and been replaced. But you don't go down to City Hall and get another birth certificate with a new name every seven years. You have a mind, but you are not your mind. Each fleeting moment you learn something new and also forget something old. Thoughts scurry through your mind without pause, though you are not your transient thoughts. You have emotions: some days you feel excited, some days you feel sad; your emotions are forever fluctuating, rising and falling like tides in the ocean, but you are not your emotions.

In the flurry of all that comes and goes in your life you are none of these transient things. Who, then, are you? Who, ever-present within your body, brings a sense of continuity and regularity into your changing world? Who shall you call your "self"? And who is it that asks, "Who am I?"

I surmised in the beginning that Consciousness descended onto the planet, and that Consciousness was love. We began by experiencing the greatest wound of all—the illusion of separation—and we forgot who we really were. The veil of forgetfulness descended upon us and we became afraid. And fear, rooted in ignorance, led us upon our journey of healing and remembering who we were—and still *are*.

By learning to accept ourselves, we heal our wounds and see more clearly the wounds of others. Slowly, we transform our resentment into forgiveness. Through forgiveness, we begin to experience compassion and empathy for the suffering of others, even if they hurt us in the past. We can see and feel that, in spite of our apparent differences, there is still a thread of commonality in the fabric of all of our lives. That thread is love. Love is all that really seems to matter—in the beginning—and in the end.

Without sufficient love, the human soul remains undernourished and is incapable of developing a healthy sense of self. Unfortunately in the mental health profession, love has rarely been emphasized as a fundamental need like food, water or shelter. In relation to human development and personal growth, love has been relegated to the back burner of importance. Yet, research has conclusively proven that infants deprived of love, physical contact and nurturing often suffer irreversible mental and emotional damage, even death.

Love is not a simple byproduct or natural outcome of early childhood conditioning. It is a necessary *precondition* for the development of a healthy self in the first place. Love is the cohesive force that consolidates the self into an integrated whole—the source of all healing, wholeness and personal well-being.

Acceptance, itself, *is* love—the "heart" of healing. Through self-acceptance, you experience the power of your loving heart in healing your wounds. You recognize that

who you really are goes well beyond the physical, emotional and mental images you have identified with in the past. You begin to love yourself whole-heartedly the way you are. Imagine how empowering it feels to realize that *you* are the love that you have been seeking.

As your head and heart come into alignment, you see more clearly through the vision of your heart. You become an expression of your own love manifesting in the world. By living your vision fully from the heart, you penetrate even further into the heart of the soul, or Psyche—your *true* birthright.

In ancient mythology, Psyche was personified as the Princess of Love. Filled with innocence and charm, she was adored and revered throughout the land. It was Psyche who infused human consciousness with the breath of life and the power of love. Prior to 1748, psychology was referred to as "the study of the soul." We have wisely adopted her name (*psych*ology) to symbolize the core of our collective identity. Psyche gracefully blended the original meaning of psychology with love, or the soul.

God, Self, the Heart, or the Seat of Consciousness, it is all the same. The point to be grasped is this, the Heart means the very core of one's being, the center, without which there is nothing whatever.

—Ramana Maharshi
East Indian Sage

Many conventional psychologists would scoff at the idea of reducing the field of psychology to "the study of the soul," or love. This notion certainly betrays the scientific precepts with which the main body of psychology has aligned itself during the past century. Yet the soul is never an object you apprehend, nor a thought you comprehend through scientific inquiry. It transcends the laws of science and mind altogether. Instead, the soul is a process that must be directly experienced, and can only be experienced through the action of loving. There is no other way, for the essence of the soul is loving.

A bell's not a bell 'til you ring it,
a song is not a song 'til you sing it.
Love in your heart wasn't put there to stay.
Love isn't love 'til you give it away!
　　　　　　—Oscar Hammerstein

You need not *search* for the soul, for the soul is not lost. You cannot *seek* self-realization, for the Self is nowhere to be sought. If you quiet your mind and listen to the silence, if you remain still and behold the blessings of the moment, you discover that "what you are looking for is what is looking."

Pause for a moment and sit with your eyes opened or closed. While focusing on your breath, observe your thoughts as they drift past like clouds passing in the sky. Don't focus on these thoughts, simply observe them as they pass by. If you find yourself following a thought as it drifts by, gently bring your awareness back to your breath, letting the thought go. Allow yourself to surrender into the emptiness between each thought.

I call this meditation *surrendering with intention*. If you practice daily, the empty space between each thought will begin to expand. Eventually, you will remain in the still, empty space of pure Awareness where your true identity as Psyche eternally resides:

All that is required to realize the Self is to be still
          —Ramana Maharshi

Your soul is not an entity you must develop, nor an object you must acquire. After stripping away all of your false identities, what remains is your True Self—or Soul— which *always has been and always shall be*. The images of the world are pale *reflections* of your True Self. Your journey of awakening, then, is the realization that you are already what you seek—where the seeker and that which is sought are one and the same.

Authentic psychotherapy literally means "healing the soul." Approached from this perspective, therapy can be highly effective in guiding us into the nature of our true identity. Rather than focusing on what's "wrong" that needs to be "fixed," we can focus on what's "right" that needs to be cultivated. Rather than numbing our pain with medications, we can foster our awareness through meditation and awaken to the splendor of our soul. We will more fully appreciate the beauty present in our lives, even in the midst of adversity. Our burdens will be transformed into blessings and we feel gratitude for the gift of life itself. We can then rejoice in the healing power of love's tender embrace.

Gratefulness is the key to joy.
Joy is the happiness that doesn't
depend on what happens.
          —Brother David Steindl-Rast, Ph.D.
          A Benedictine Monk

In closing, let's turn again to the power of imagination. Imagine the comfort that arises from cultivating empathy, kindness and compassion. Imagine these qualities being shared amongst all human beings. Imagine as you touch—and are touched by—the hearts of others, you experience unconditional love for one another. Imagine discovering that beneath the veneer of separation, there is only *One Consciousness*. As we experience this One Consciousness, imagine we are *all* contributing to healing the planet as a whole. Imagine *love*.

Imagine all the people sharing all the world.
You may say I'm a dreamer, but I'm not the only one.
I hope someday you'll join us and the world will live
　　As one.
　　　　　　—John Lennon

Afterword

Now that you have journeyed through the human drama, I want to share with you how this book came into being. I have worked as a therapist and educator for over thirty years and have been actively involved with a variety of mental health and substance abuse programs throughout northern California. I have encountered a wide range of people and situations, from everyday life struggles to major trauma and abuse. This work has been both rewarding and challenging. I have gained a lot from these experiences, which I have tried to integrate in a manner that would assist, guide, and teach others.

In 1990 I was asked to give a workshop on self-esteem at a county mental health conference. At the time, my wife Carol and I were in the middle of building our house. All of our belongings, including my notes and materials on the subject of self-esteem, were packed away in a little shed on our property. We slept in the back of our pickup truck, took solar showers and lived in a small space in a part of the shed that wasn't packed with furniture.

Being consumed by the building process and not having access to my material, I was about to decline the offer. Instead, I was suddenly struck with the idea of resurrecting a favorite past time, doodling with cartoons. Whenever I attend workshops I surreptitiously doodle cartoons all over my note paper, so why not do the same thing while *presenting* a workshop?" I ran down to a local art supply store and bought an easel pad, flow pens and colored pencils.

I soon found myself on the floor of our six by ten living space each night drawing color cartoons. By the time the workshop date arrived, I had completed fifteen to twenty cartoons. The illustrations served as an outline for the workshop as well as visual aids for the participants. Each cartoon represented a topic of discussion, which was followed by an interpersonal process, to give participants a hands-on experience of the subject matter presented. The workshop was a success; the participants were enthusiastic and loved the cartoons. Afterward, I stored the drawings away and went back to building the house.

About ten years later, I began facilitating self-acceptance and forgiveness workshops at Esalen Institute near Big Sur, California. At one point, I remembered the cartoons stored away in my closet, and decided to bring them along in case they might be useful. On the fourth day of the five-day workshop, I presented the cartoons as a way to review the week and to add some comic relief from the intense personal work that participants had experienced.

Again, the workshop was a success and the participants got a big kick out of the cartoons. For my next workshop six months later, I drew more cartoons, pictures I hoped would reflect the common struggles we face as part of the human drama. These new cartoons generated even more laughter, and once again, offered us all a welcomed reprieve from the intensity of the week.

I was now hooked on doodling with cartoons again. I was also combining it with the other thing I loved most—assisting people in their own personal growth. As each new workshop date arrived, I added an additional set of cartoons to my repertoire.

In October 2002 at an Esalen workshop, I once again presented the cartoons, which now consisted of about fifty laminated pictures. Afterwards, one of the participants approached me. Referring to the cartoons, he commented, "I think you have a book there." I laughed and told him I already had a book-length manuscript in my closet and had given up looking for a publisher. He replied, "Well I *am* a publisher," and he expressed an interest in publishing the

cartoons primarily as an illustrated story rather than creating a full-blown text on personal growth and healing.

But as I began working on this project, it soon became apparent that I could not effectively present the cartoons without a good deal of accompanying text to put them in perspective—I needed a narrative to match the flavor of the cartoons. I began writing, and soon found myself drawing *more* cartoons to match the growing text. Each cartoon generated new thoughts and each new idea generated more cartoons. As I oscillated between text and cartoons, I began to panic. This cycle could continue indefinitely unless I found a way to bring it to an end—an ending that took another seven chapters to complete! Part three of the book represents this ending, and is comprised primarily of the tools necessary for personal growth and healing.

In reviewing the material, I saw that the central focus of the preceding text was a portrayal of our daily struggles, issues of self-esteem, personal effectiveness and a search for identity—what now constitutes part two of the book. I realized there was no beginning to the story—how the human drama got started in the first place. Back to the drawing board I went, and part one was born.

But something crucial was still missing, something that preceded our familiar context altogether. If I reached far enough, could I give a glimpse of what that essence was—

or is—*prior* to the beginning? This essence, I believe, transcends the boundaries of time and space completely. My attempt to portray this "eternal now," the essence of what "is, was, and forevermore shall be," was integrated into the introduction to the book.

Finally, once it dawned on me that these cartoons were actually going to be published, I panicked again. I redrew twenty of the originals. I ended up with a total of about seventy old and new. Each cartoon took four to six hours to complete. They were drawn and colored by hand on a large easel pad. The finished color cartoons are two feet by three feet in size, big enough for public display.

Tackling this project and bringing it to completion has been laborious, but clearly a labor of love. I feel blessed to have been able to bring my favorite skills together into a meaningful whole and share them with you in the form of this book. I hope you enjoyed both the text and the cartoons as much as I have enjoyed putting them together.

With peace, joy and laughter,
Joseph Cavanaugh

Bibliography

References:

Part One
Chapter 1
The Spirit of Science. Edited by David Lorimer Continuum Publishing Company, 1998.

Chapter 4
Psycho-Cybernetics by Maxwell Maltz, M.D. Simon & Schuster, 1960.

Part Two
Chapter 5
Becoming Attached by Robert Karen, Ph.D. Oxford University Press, 1998.

A General Theory of Love by Thomas Lewis, M.D., Fari Amini, M.D. and Richard Lannon, M.D. Random House, N.Y.

The Biology of Transcendence by Joseph Chilton. Pearce Park Street Press, 2002.

Drama of the Gifted Child by Alice Miller. Basic Books, Inc. 1981.

Healing the Shame That Binds You by John Bradshaw. Health Communications, 1998

Chapter 7
For Your Own Good by Alice Miller. The Noonday Press, 1990.

Chapter 9
Emotional Intelligence by Daniel Goleman. Bantam Books, 1995.

Part Three
Chapter 13
The Emotional Brain by Joseph LeDoux, Ph.D. Simon & Schuster, 1996.

Chapter 14
Forgive for Good by Fred Luskin, Ph.D. HarperCollins Paperback Edition, 2003

Recommended Reading

Actualizations by Stewart Emery

A General Theory of Love by Thomas Lewis, M.D., Fari Amini, M.D. and Richard Lannon, M.D.

A Path with Heart by Jack Kornfield

Becoming Attached by Robert Karen, Ph.D.

Drama of the Gifted Child by Alice Miller

Emotional Intelligence by Daniel Goleman

Forgive for Good by Fred Luskin, Ph.D.

For Your Own Good by Alice Miller

Gratefulness, the Heart of Prayer by Brother David Steindl-Rast

Healing the Shame That Binds You by John Bradshaw

Ideas and Opinions by Albert Einstein

On Becoming a Leader by Warren Bennis

Psycho-cybernetics by Maxwell Maltz, M.D.

Recovering the Soul by Larry Dossey, M.D.

Return to Love by Marianne Williamson

Stories of the Spirit, Stories of the Heart by Feldman and Kornfield

The Biology of Transcendence by Joseph Chilton Pearce

The Emotional Brain by Joseph Ledoux, Ph.D.

The Evolution of Consciousness by Robert Ornstein

The Guru Papers by Joel Kramer and Diana Alstad

The Holographic Universe by Michael Talbot

The Portable Jung edited by Joseph Campbell

The Power of Myth by Joseph Campbell

The Search for the Real Self by James Masterson, M.D.

The Seat of the Soul by Gary Zukav

The Spectrum of Consciousness by Ken Wilber

The Spirit of Science edited by David Lorimer

The Spiritual Teachings of Ramana Maharshi foreworded by Carl Jung

The Tao of Physics by Fritjof Capra

The Wisdom of No Escape by Pema Chodron

Tuesdays with Morrie by Mitch Albom

About the Author

Joseph Cavanaugh has been working in the field of mental health since 1970. He received his master's degree in counseling from California State University, San Francisco. He is licensed as a Marriage and Family Therapist, and works with individuals and couples in his private practice.

Joe was employed with the Department of Rehabilitation for 25 years as a mental health and substance abuse counselor. He ran groups with recovering alcoholics, substance abusers and legal offenders on parole. Over the years, he has conducted workshops on self-awareness, self-esteem, relationships and personal effectiveness. His cartoons have been published in *Runners World* and *Triathlete* magazines.

He currently facilitates self-acceptance workshops at Esalen Institute in Big Sur, California. He is an adjunct professor at Sierra College where he has taught courses in psychology, personal development and social science. He lives in the Sierra foothills of northern California with his wife Carol and their dog Daisy, and currently has three grown children and two grandchildren.